KEY CONCEPTS IN PUBLIC RELATIONS

D0130461

Palgrave Key Concepts

Palgrave Key Concepts provide an accessible and comprehensive range of subject glossaries at undergraduate level. They are the ideal companion to a standard textbook making them invaluable reading to students through-out their course of study and especially useful as a revision aid.

Key Concepts in Accounting and Finance
Key Concepts in Business Practice
Key Concepts in Cultural Studies
Key Concepts in Drama and Performance
Key Concepts in e-Commerce
Key Concepts in Human Resource Management
Key Concepts in Information and Communication Technology
Key Concepts in International Business
Key Concepts in Language and Linguistics (second edition)
Key Concepts in Law
Key Concepts in Leisure
Key Concepts in Management
Key Concepts in Marketing
Key Concepts in Operations Management
Key Concepts in Politics
Key Concepts in Public Relations
Key Concepts in Psychology
Key Concepts in Social Research Methods
Key Concepts in Sociology
Key Concepts in Strategic Management
Key Concepts in Tourism

Palgrave Key Concepts: Literature

General Editors: John Peck and Martin Coyle

Key Concepts in Contemporary Literature
Key Concepts in Crime Fiction
Key Concepts in Medieval Literature
Key Concepts in Modernist Literature
Key Concepts in Postcolonial Literature
Key Concepts in Renaissance Literature
Key Concepts in Victorian Literature
Literary Terms and Criticism (third edition)

Further titles are in preparation
www.palgravekeyconcepts.com

Palgrave Key Concepts
Series Standing Order
ISBN 1–4039–3210–7
(outside North America only)

You can receive future titles in this series as they are published by placing a standing order. Please contact your bookseller or, in the case of difficulty, write to us at the address below with your name and address, the title of the series and the ISBN quoted above.

Customer Services Department, Macmillan Distribution Ltd
Houndmills, Basingstoke, Hampshire RG21 6XS, England

Key Concepts in Public Relations

Sandra Cain

palgrave
macmillan

© Sandra Cain 2009

All rights reserved. No reproduction, copy or transmission of this publication may be made without written permission.

No portion of this publication may be reproduced, copied or transmitted save with written permission or in accordance with the provisions of the Copyright, Designs and Patents Act 1988, or under the terms of any licence permitting limited copying issued by the Copyright Licensing Agency, Saffron House, 6-10 Kirby Street, London EC1N 8TS.

Any person who does any unauthorized act in relation to this publication may be liable to criminal prosecution and civil claims for damages.

The author has asserted her right to be identified as the author of this work in accordance with the Copyright, Designs and Patents Act 1988.

First published 2009 by
PALGRAVE MACMILLAN

Palgrave Macmillan in the UK is an imprint of Macmillan Publishers Limited, registered in England, company number 785998, of Houndmills, Basingstoke, Hampshire RG21 6XS.

Palgrave Macmillan in the US is a division of St Martin's Press LLC, 175 Fifth Avenue, New York, NY 10010.

Palgrave Macmillan is the global academic imprint of the above companies and has companies and representatives throughout the world.

Palgrave® and Macmillan® are registered trademarks in the United States, the United Kingdom, Europe and other countries.

ISBN-13: 978-0-230-20329-7
ISBN-10: 0-230-20329-9

This book is printed on paper suitable for recycling and made from fully managed and sustained forest sources. Logging, pulping and manufacturing processes are expected to conform to the environmental regulations of the country of origin.

A catalogue record for this book is available from the British Library.

A catalog record for this book is available from the Library of Congress.

10 9 8 7 6 5 4 3 2 1
18 17 16 15 14 13 12 11 10 09

Printed and bound in Great Britain by
CPI Antony Rowe, Chippenham and Eastbourne

Contents

Figures

Tables

Introduction

The Chartered Institute of Public Relations (CIPR) claims that public relations is currently the third most desirable graduation destination. Although public relations **techniques** have been used in different forms for centuries, public relations itself is often referred to as a new, emerging and young business profession. The purpose of public relations is to create understanding between an organisation and its various **stakeholders** and is important because it stresses the need for planning, sustained effort and **mutual understanding**. Both the theory of public relations and its practice borrow from several other disciplines, notably marketing, advertising, sociology, psychology and communications. In 1976 Rex Harlow ('Building a public relations definition', *Public Relations Review*, 4, 2, 34–42) examined 472 definitions of public relations and came up with the following definition to explain what public relations *does*.

> Public relations is a distinctive management function which helps establish and maintain mutual lines of communication, understanding, acceptance and co-operation between an organisation and its **publics**; involves the management of problems or **issue**s; helps management to keep informed on and responsive to **public opinion**; defines and emphasises the responsibility of management to serve the public interest; helps management keep abreast of and efficiently utilise change, serving as an early warning system to help anticipate trends: and uses research and ethical communication **techniques** as its principal **tools**.

A simpler statement which best spells out the full role, nature and responsibilities of the public relations function is that cited by F. C. Jefkins in 1994: 'Public Relations practice is the art and social science of analysing trends, predicting their consequences, counselling organisation leaders, and implementing planned programmes of action that will serve both the organisations and the public interest' (*Public Relations Techniques*, 2nd edn. Oxford: Butterworth-Heinemann).

Public relations tells the organisation's 'story' – its narrative – to its **stakeholders** and other interested parties. It also helps to shape and change the organisation and the way it works in practice for the benefit of itself, its environment and its **publics**. Effective public relations helps to manage reputation – an organisation's greatest asset. It is 'about reputation – the result of what you do, what you say and what others say about you' (CIPR).

Public relations is in its ascendancy. Globally, public relations professionals are being employed in every walk of life from the voluntary sector and **pressure groups** to multi-national organisations, political organisations, business leaders and smaller organisations. Today there is much debate between those who view public relations as a management function and those who deem it primarily in relationship to the media. One of the most useful definitions of public relations is that given by the CIPR in 1987: 'Public Relations is the planned and sustained effort to establish and maintain goodwill and understanding between an organisation and its publics.'

The words 'planned' and 'sustained' suggest that good relationships are not a given but need to be planned for and worked at. In effect this definition crystallises the idea that public relations is ongoing, strategic and interactive and not a series of unrelated events or happenings. However, there are still many people – members of the general public, practitioners and scholars – who are confused about what public relations *is*. This is evident in job advertisements where public relations is often advertised as corporate communications, **image** management, even as perception management. But public relations is fast building its own body of knowledge and scholarship and the number of universities now offering courses in public relations at both undergraduate and post-graduate level is increasing yearly.

As the title suggests, *Key Concepts in Public Relations* attempts to deliver the main concepts for consideration in the field of public relations. However, because public relations draws on so many other disciplines, it is impossible to define all the terms applicable without straying too much into the fields of **marketing**, advertising, psychology and sociology and away from the main branch and scholarship of public relations itself. The book will inevitably detail concepts which some may find inapplicable and omit others which some consider applicable. I have, therefore, included those concepts that I, both as a practitioner and scholar, consider the most pertinent and useful, and I hope that readers will agree with me.

The key concepts are arranged in alphabetical order for ease of access and understanding. Each concept is explained briefly and then expanded upon where necessary. Some of the concepts within the text refer to other concepts. In each case these are highlighted in **bold** type. Readers can then refer directly to these supporting concepts for further information or clarification. Many of the key concepts are also followed by references to further reading or to websites. Each of these allows the reader to follow up with further research.

'Key Concepts in Public Relations' provides a valuable resource both to the new public relations practitioner wishing to know more about the terms, facts and concepts which affect their craft and also to the student of public relations wishing to be introduced to outlines of more theoretical and scholarly ideas.

Diagrams of various public relations and communication concepts and models drawn to simplify the ideas are also included in the text.

Sandra Cain

Above the line

'Above the line' and '**below the line**' are marketing terms. **Promotion** or **advertising** of a product or service using media such as television, radio, magazines and newspapers is known as above the line because this type of **promotion** requires commission to be paid to an **advertising** agency in contrast to **public relations**, **marketing** and **promotion**s which are regarded as **below the line**. The 'line' is an imaginary line between those **advertising** media which pay commission to **advertising** agencies and those which do not. Recently the division between above the line and below the line has become indistinct.

ACCA

ACCA (<u>A</u>wareness, <u>C</u>omprehension, <u>C</u>onviction, <u>A</u>ction) is part of the **motivating sequence**.

Consumers are first made aware that the product or service exists. They must then comprehend what the product or service is about and how it will benefit them. Customers must then be convinced to buy the product or service and finally they must take action and either buy the product or engage with the service.

See **AIDA model, four Ps, motivating sequence.**

Active publics

Active publics are a subset of an organisation's overall **publics**. They are groups of people who do something about a **public relations** problem. For example, if a local factory expands its business and causes an increase in local traffic levels, the community may decide to blockade the factory gates or write letters of complaint to the local press. Active publics can be divided into three further categories: **all-issue publics, single-issue publics** and **hot-issue publics**.

Activism

Activism is intentional action by a group of people to bring about social, organisational or political change. **Pressure groups**, interest groups or citizen groups of activists are formed when two or more people organise on behalf of a cause to exert pressure on an organisation to change the way it functions. Activists are motivated by a desire to correct apparent injustices, for example the abuse of worker, animal or human rights, or when they perceive danger, for example damage to the environment or to the nation's health. Activism against an organisation can at best damage and at worst ruin its **reputation** and activists therefore have to be handled sensitively. Organisations most at **risk** from activists include manufacturing operations, especially those with pollution potential, organisations carrying out **research** on animals, e.g. universities and pharmaceutical companies, those whose products, for example GM foods, vaccines, CFCs and tobacco, are perceived as damaging, and organisations whose activities, for example mining, farming, oil exploration and refining and nuclear power plants, are regarded as damaging. All democratic governments and publicly quoted companies are open to shareholder activism. Recognising the potential for activism against an organisation forms part of the **public relations issues planning** or **boundary scanning** process. If an organisation is targeted by activists, it must engage in **crisis management**.

Deegan (2001) suggests that the dynamics of activism are thus:

- Activists represent a growing threat to organisations in an increasingly pluralistic society.
- They use a wide range of **tactics** including direct pressure on those targeted as well as seeking media, public, regulatory and government intervention. More recently activists are targeting financial institutions which fund certain organisations.
- Regardless of the **tactics** used or the length or the severity of the resulting conflict, activists disrupt those they target.
- It is the organisation to a large extent which determines how aggressive or co-operative activists will be.
- Activists are more likely to co-operate with organisations which are open to **negotiation**.
- Organisations which learn how to deal effectively with activists improve their functioning in a broader sense.

A

Deegan suggests that **public relations** practitioners and communications specialists should not:

- ignore activists because this increases the likelihood that they will seek third-party intervention from the media, the government and the public to force change – avoiding **issues** encourages them to spiral out of control;
- seek to influence **public opinion** in response to activist pressure because it is extremely difficult to change people's behaviour and **attitudes**, especially in turbulent environments;
- adopt aggressive behaviour, such as trying to discredit groups, initiating lawsuits against them or seeking to undermine their funding, as this is likely to require endless financial and human **resources** – groups prosper when threatened and an organisation's reputation can be badly damaged by being publicly presented as a bully;
- seek to persuade activists of the 'bigger picture' – this has limited effect as activists resist being persuaded.

Deegan suggests a way forward in dealing with activists. She claims that the views of activists and organisations are not as disparate as either side believes – it is a lack of trust which keeps them apart. She claims that activists are less likely to be aggressive or seek third-party involvement if the targeted organisation takes a co-operative stance and adopts **two-way symmetrical communication** based on proactive **negotiation** and **conflict resolution**. The emphasis of **negotiation** should be based on building lasting relationships with activists and response and adjustment to their changing views. **Research** into the organisation's changing environment and the development of a strategic communications plan are key elements of **two-way symmetrical communication**. Ongoing **evaluation** helps to keep the plan effective and relevant.

See **conflict resolution, negotiation, win–win**.

Deegan, D. (2001) *Managing Activism*. London: Kogan Page.

A

Advertising

Advertising is the paid-for, one-way **message** or set of communications from a sponsor via the media to an **audience**. Advertising promotes a product to an existing customer or to a potential customer. Advertising is part of the **marketing** programme and is often used to support the **public relations programme/plan**. Advertising creates a desire to buy and relies on sending **messages** about the **features** and **benefits** of a product, a service, a cultural artefact or a lifestyle.

The Institute of Practitioners in Advertising defines advertising as: 'the management process responsible for identifying, anticipating and satisfying customer requirements profitably'.

See **AIDA model, marketing.**

Burtenshaw, K., Mahon, N. and Barfoot, C. (2007) *The Fundamentals of Creative Advertising*. Switzerland: Ava Publishing.
www.ipa.co.uk

Advertising Standards Authority (ASA)

The ASA is the independent British self-regulatory organisation of the **advertising** industry. It is funded by a charge on the advertising industry, thereby operating a system of self-regulation. The ASA's purpose is to support best practice in **advertising** by ensuring that it is 'legal, honest and truthful'.

www.asa.org.uk

Advertorials

Advertorials might be regarded as a cross between an advertisement and a newsworthy **press release**. When **advertising** space is sold in a magazine or other publication, an advertorial in the shape of a feature article is run alongside it. Advertorials can include advertisements for a **brand** masked as an **editorial** or as a **feature article** recommending a **brand** name. Rules have been introduced to counter this misuse of **journalist**ic licence. 'Reader advertisements' written in a **journalist**ic style resembling **editorial** copy must be distinguished by the words, 'Advertisement' or 'Advertiser's Announcement' in compliance with the British Code of Advertising Practice. Similar advertorials featured on television or radio are known as **infomercials**.

Advisory fees

Advisory fees cover consultancy advice, attending meetings, preparing reports and **proposals**, etc. This is normally based on a fixed amount of time per month and paid to a **public relations** practitioner or **consultancy** on a retainer basis or on a project basis.

Agenda-setting theory

Agenda-setting theory is the theory that the **mass media** influence **audience**s by acting as a framing device and choosing which

A

stories they consider newsworthy and by how much coverage and prominence they give them. **Public relations** practitioners often work with the media to put an organisation's message about an **issue** or programme forward and so make it salient to the **audience**. It is generally accepted that **journalist**s set the news agenda and therefore relay which narratives the public should be conscious of – the notion of agenda-setting relies on the transfer of **issue**s from the media to the public. Studies by McCombs and Shaw (1972) and Rogers and Dearing (1988) focused on awareness and information within agenda-setting. They investigated the agenda-setting function of the **mass media** in the 1968 presidential campaign and attempted to assess the relationship between what voters in one community said were important **issue**s and the actual content of media **messages** used during the campaign. They concluded that the **mass media** exerted a significant influence on what voters considered to be the major **issue**s of the campaign.

McCombs, M. E. and Shaw, D. L. (1972) 'The agenda-setting function in the mass media', *Public Opinion Quarterly*, 36 (Summer), 176–187.

Rogers, E. M. and Dearing, J. W. (1988) 'Agenda-setting research: Where has it been, where is it going?', in J. A. Anderson (ed.) *Communication Yearbook* 11, 555–594. Newbury Park, CA: Sage.

AIDA model

AIDA (create A̲wareness, generate I̲nterest, develop D̲esire, initiate A̲ction) is a purpose and flow **marketing** and **promotion**al term, also used by PR practitioners. Initially people become A̲ware of an idea or product or service but have little knowledge about it. Then they develop an I̲nterest and seek out more information. Then they become persuaded of the **benefits** of the idea or product or service and develop a D̲esire to buy it. Finally they show their support by taking A̲ction and buying the product or service.

See **ACCA, BFD formula, four Ps, motivating sequence.**

A

All-issue publics

All-issue publics are a subset of an organisation's overall **publics** and are a further division of an organisation's **active publics**. They are groups of people who are active on all **issue**s affecting an organisation. They may well be opposed to the organisation in principle and be prepared to disrupt all of its activities. It is important for **public relations** practitioners to consider this group of **publics** very carefully in their **issues management** planning.

See **publics.**

Ambient media

Ambient media is the use of non-traditional or alternative media. It uses unusual settings to convey a message, such as projections on to buildings, messages on the back of car park receipts or on supermarket trolleys, **slogans** on hot air balloons, giant posters on the sides of trucks, messages via Bluetooth, advertisements on cash machines, etc. There has been a growth in the use of ambient media recently owing to its general versatility, a decline in the power of traditional media and a greater demand for **point of sale** communications. New technology has also revolutionised outdoor media, producing improved targeting, reduced costs and greater accountability. Ambient advertisements are very effective at pushing **messages** into the consciousness of consumers, particularly when the **audience** is specifically targeted. Ambient media can produce mass attention and focus in centralised locations or can be used to interact directly with consumers when they are involved in everyday activities such as shopping or travelling.

White, R. (2004) 'Ambient media – best practice', *Admap*, Oct.

Ambush marketing

Ambush marketing can be considered an exploitation of the **sponsorship** often associated with major sporting events such as the World Cup or the Olympics. Here an official sponsor has to compete with an unauthorised **publicity** seeker. Ambush marketers will find ways to communicate **messages** about their products through a wide range of unpaid-for **marketing** activities and will ultimately succeed in deflecting some of the attention away from the official sponsor on to themselves.

Analysis

Analysis is the first stage in the planning cycle of a **public relations programme/plan**. It entails **research** into **issue**s which will affect the overall plan and looks at both the **micro environment** and the **macro environment**. Analysis includes both a **PEST analysis** and a **SWOT analysis**.

Analysis and **research** can be done by either in-house **researchers** or external **researchers** and can be either **qualitative** or **quantitative**. **Primary research** involves finding out the required information first-hand and can include **questionnaires,** one-to-one **interviews, telephone interviews, focus groups, internet groups, media research** and **communication audits**.

Gregory, A. (2004) *Planning and Managing Public Relations Campaigns*. London: Kogan Page.

Annual General Meeting (AGM)

An AGM is held once a year to inform an organisation's interested parties and members about their previous and future activities. It is an opportunity for members to ask questions relating to finances and any decisions the organisation will take in the future. It is an important meeting for the **public relations** manager who will have had input in the writing of the **Annual Report** presented at the AGM.

Annual Report

An Annual Report is a document often written or overseen by the **public relations** practitioner. A company presents its Annual Report at the **Annual General Meeting (AGM)** for approval by its shareholders. An Annual Report is made up of financial reports and other reports including the Chairman's report and the organisation's **mission statement**.

Apathetic publics

Apathetic publics is the term James **Grunig** gave to a group of people he defined as not really **publics** at all. These people have no interest in the organisation. However, it can be argued that as a subset they are important to **public relations** practitioners for their *potential* to become more engaged.

> *See* **publics**.

Aristotle

Aristotle (384-322 BC) was a Greek philosopher. He wrote on such diverse subjects as physics, metaphysics, poetry, logic, **rhetoric**, politics, government, **ethics**, biology and zoology. He is often cited as being the first and foremost authority on communication. His work on **rhetoric** – the influencing and persuading of others through the spoken word – developed in democratic Greece and his thoughts are highly influential today. Many contemporary politicians, speech-writers and speech-makers depend on the **techniques** he advocated, especially the 'triple', as used by Tony Blair in his 'education, education, education' speech. Aristotle suggested that communication consisted of three elements:

- *ethos*: the nature or qualities of the communicator;
- *logos*: the nature, structure and content of the message itself;
- *pathos*: the nature, feelings and thoughts of the receiver or **audience**.

A

Hiltunen, A. (2002) *Aristotle in Hollywood, the Anatomy of Successful Storytelling*. Bristol: Intellect Books.

Articles

Also known as **feature articles**, or features, an article is a 'story' written exclusively for one publication. Articles are written in a different style to **press release**s and have a strong narrative flow. Articles take time to prepare, **research** and write. The writer needs to renegotiate with the publication's editor, check and recheck drafts and sources and prepare images. Articles are written by an authority on a subject and are often kept as reference material. They are an excellent way for a **public relations** practitioner to communicate **messages** to readers. All articles need a theme, idea or subject. Articles should never be written speculatively. The chosen theme needs to be strong enough to persuade the editor of the publication to publish.

Once the writer has thought out the ideas for the article and worked out the preliminaries, he/she needs to propose the article to the editor. The **proposal** letter should include:

- the idea (theme)
- any clearances obtained or to be obtained for permission to publish
- any clearance for **research**.

Once the publisher commissions the idea, the writer needs the following information in order to proceed:

- the word count
- any special treatments needed
- the type and number of illustrations or images
- the **issue** date of publication
- the copy dates and deadlines
- the fees.

When writing the actual article, the writer should consider the following:

- the opening paragraph or lead-in – the beginning should lead into the body of the article;
- the previous or present situation – and any related problems;
- the search for a solution – the 'core' of the article;
- the solution and results achieved – how it was done;
- the closing paragraph – with a summary and perhaps 'a look ahead' or 'a way forward'.

A well-**research**ed, well-written and illustrated feature article is an excellent form of **public relations** and benefits the organisation, its products and its business.

Hennessy, B. (2004) *Writing Feature Articles*, 4th edn. Oxford: Focal Press.

Associated Press

The Associated Press is an American global news network. It is the world's largest news agency and is a co-operative owned by its contributing newspapers, radio and television stations who all contribute to it and use material written by its staffers. It is accessed by **public relations** professionals all over the world.

Asymmetrical communication

Unlike **symmetrical communication**, asymmetrical communication flows one way from sender to receiver and is considered to be a **closed system**. Asymmetrical communication methods generally focus on achieving short-term attitude change and are used by organisations primarily interested in having their **publics** come around to their way of thinking rather than the organisation changing itself, its policies or its views. The asymmetrical model of communication is supported by several presuppositions:

- there is an inability to see the organisation as outsiders do (internal orientation);
- information flows out but not in (**closed system**);
- the control of cost is more important than innovation (efficiency);
- the leader of the organisation is considered to know best (elitism);
- there is a **resistance** to change (conservatism);
- there is a desire for tradition, to keep the organisation 'together';
- there is central authority (no autonomy for employees).

See **Grunig's four models of public relations, symmetrical communication, systems theory.**

Attitudes

A

Schiffman and Kanuk (1996) claim that attitudes are a learned predisposition to behave in a consistently favourable or unfavourable way with respect to a given object. Attitudes are mental constructs or thoughts. They are learned and developed through experience, and as such are fluid and changing. They are not directly observable yet are the key to successful **persuasion**. Because individuals are favourably inclined towards an object or they are not, attitudes are therefore deemed to be *evaluative*. Attitudes have two components: **beliefs** and **values**.

See **attitude formation.**

Cain, S. and Maxwell, M. (2004) *How to Get What You Want: Unlock the Magic of Your Mind and Achieve Your Goals*. Oxford: How To Books.

Schiffman, L. G. and Kanuk, L. (1996) *Consumer Behaviour*, 6th edn. Englewood Cliffs, NJ: Prentice Hall.

Attitude formation

American academics, Cutlip, Center and Broom (2000) claim that **public relations** is about changing or neutralising hostile opinions and **attitudes**, crystallising uninformed or latent opinions and **attitudes** or conserving favourable opinions and **attitudes**. Attitude formation is a continuous process. As knowledge and experience blend with existing **attitudes**, modified **attitudes** then emerge. Former **research** carried out in order to design the **public relations programme/plan** will have indicated the **attitudes** formed by various **publics** and **audience**s. It is far easier to strengthen favourable opinions than it is to counteract hostile ones. **Attitudes** can be formed by several influences, including first-hand knowledge of a situation or **issue**, second-hand knowledge via the media and other formal communications, social conditioning and commonly held **beliefs**. There is a strong link between **beliefs**, **values** and **attitudes**. What one believes, or the **values** that one holds, will have a direct correlation with one's attitude towards a person, product, **issue** or organisation. However, it is important to acknowledge that **beliefs** are not necessarily 'true'; they are merely constructs and as such can be changed, thereby changing **attitudes** accordingly.

The main characteristics of **attitudes** and their formation is that they are:

- *learned* – through personal experience, through information provided by others or by exposure to the **mass media**;
- *predisposed* – a predisposition is a tendency towards something, so attitudes have motivational qualities;
- *linked to behaviour* – behaviour of **publics** is of primary interest to **public relations** practitioners;
- *consistent* – but not necessarily permanent;
- *directed towards an object and are reactions to that object* – for example a person may like 'x' but not 'y';
- *situationally determined* – a person may like a glass of wine with dinner, for example, but not with breakfast.

See **attitudes, beliefs, values.**

Cutlip, S. M., Centre, A. H. and Broom, G. M. (2000) *Effective Public Relations*, 8th edn. Upper Saddle River, NJ: Prentice-Hall.

A

Fishbein, M. (1973) 'The prediction of behaviour from attitudinal variables', in C. D. Mortenson and K. Sereno (eds) *Advances in Communication Research*. New York: Harper and Row.

Attribution theory

Attribution theory is concerned with the way in which people explain (attribute) the behaviour of others or themselves with something else. It looks at how individuals attribute causes to events and how this perception affects their motivation. The theory divides the factors into two types:

1. External or situational attribution assigns causality to an outside factor such as the weather or a traffic jam on the motorway.
2. Internal or dispositional attribution assigns causality to factors within people themselves, such as their competence or other variables which make the individual responsible for the event.

People often make self-serving attributions, so if something good happens they may attribute it to internal factors, whereas if something bad happens they often blame external factors. Attributions for events can alter a person's behaviour and many theories such as **cognitive dissonance** rely on it. Coombs (1998) used attribution theory to explain and predict people's perceptions of **crises** and the impact of **crises** on an organisation's **reputation**. There are three causal triggers which affect the development of attribution:

- *Stability* – this indicates whether an event happens frequently (stable) or infrequently (unstable). The more stable the event, the stronger the attributions of the individual's responsibility for an event.
- *External control* – this constitutes the extent to which an event is controlled by some outside factor. Stronger external control promotes attributions that the situation is responsible for the event.
- *Personal control* – this reflects a person's intentions and/or ability to control an event. Increased perceptions of personal control promote attributions of an individual's responsibility for the event.

A

Coombs, W. T. (1998) 'An analytic framework for crisis situations: Better responses from a better understanding of the situation', *Journal of Public Relations Research*, 10, 177–191.

Audience-profiling

Audience-profiling is the term given to the task of identifying the key characteristics of readers, viewers or listeners of either print or **broadcast media**. Information on profiles is gathered through **market research** and then used to target **marketing**, **advertising** or **public relations messages**.

See **audience**.

Audience

Audiences are made up of the groups of people or individuals to whom various **messages** about the organisation are communicated. In **public relations** terms they are called **publics**.

See **publics**.

Aware publics

Aware publics are a subset of an organisation's overall **publics**. They are groups of people who recognise that a **public relations** problem or **issue** exists. They may have read about it in the newspapers, seen the problem on television or have been told about it directly.

Awareness campaign

An awareness campaign is a **public relations** campaign designed to create awareness and knowledge about a product or service which may not necessarily result in sales. It is a method of introducing and educating the public about an **issue**, product or service.

See **public relations programme/plan**.

A

Backgrounders

Backgrounders are sheets sent with the **press pack** which provide more detailed and in-depth information on the organisation. Typically they can include a history of the organisation, an outline of its **organisational structure**, charts and graphs for providing statistical information, fact sheets, **brochures**, **newsletter**s, press clips and **articles**, biographies of organisational leaders, photographs (product, location, organisational characters, etc.), product information, case histories, etc.

Balance theory

Balance theory is a motivational theory of attitude change suggested by Fritz Heider (1946) which uses the motive of consistency as a drive towards psychological balance. Balance theory is about the receipt of information: 'balance' occurs if a person is reassured about his/her (either negative or positive) **attitude** towards an object when it is compared with the attitude of another person. For example, balance occurs when another declares a similar **attitude** towards the object. Heider was interested in the ways in which people view their relations with other people and their environment. The **analysis** centred on two people labelled **P** and **O**, where **P** was the focus of the **analysis** and **O** represented some other person. An impersonal entity (an idea, an event, an object) was labelled **X**. Heider sought to discover how relations between **P, O** and **X** were organised in **P**'s cognitive structure and whether these were systematic tendencies.

However, this simplistic explanation does not fully explain the complexities involved because it works on a straight positive or negative aspect without considering the varying strengths of those **attitudes**. Balance theory is useful in examining how celebrity **endorsement** affects consumers' **attitudes** towards products or services. If a person admires the celebrity and perceives (as a result of the advertisement) that the celebrity likes the product or service, the person will tend to like the product or service more in order to achieve psychological balance. However, if a person already had a dislike for the product or service being endorsed by the celebrity, he/she may begin to like the celebrity less as well as liking the product or service more in order to achieve psychological balance. In order to successfully predict the likely outcome of a situation using Heider's balance theory, one must measure all the effects of the potential results: the one requiring the least effort will be the most likely outcome. Some imbalance is tolerable, resulting in parties simply agreeing to disagree. Newcomb advanced Heider's balance theory in 1953 by taking Heider's notion of balance out of one person's head and applying it to communication among a mass of people.

See **cognitive dissonance, congruity theory.**

Heider, F. (1946) 'Attitudes and cognitive organisation', *Journal of Psychology*, 21, 107–112.
Newcomb, T. M. (1953) 'An approach to the study of communicative acts', *Psychological Review*, 60, 393–404.

BARB

BARB (the Broadcaster's Audience Research Board) is the name of the organisation which compiles television ratings in the UK. The organisation places approximately 5,500 boxes in homes around the country which record which channels the householders are watching. These numbers are reported back to the television stations and advertisers. BARB numbers are important to commercial television stations because the trading model depends on the level of viewing: the **advertising** agency pays the television studio an amount of money depending on the number of people watching a certain show. The higher the BARB numbers, the more money a television station will make.

BBC

The BBC (British Broadcasting Corporation) is the largest broadcasting corporation in the world in terms of **audience** numbers and revenue, with a **budget** of £4 billion. The corporation produces programmes and information services, broadcasting globally on television, radio and the internet. The stated mission of the BBC is to 'inform, educate and entertain', while its motto is 'Nation shall speak peace unto nation'. The BBC operates as a public service broadcaster, claiming that it is 'free from both political and commercial influence and answers only to its viewers and listeners'. Its domestic programming and broadcasts are funded by a licence fee.

www.bbc.co.uk

Belbin's team roles

Belbin (1993) identifies nine team roles which he suggests determine the performance of a group. As much of **public relations** involves team work, these team roles can be an important matter for consideration and could provide **public relations** managers with the ability to design specially selected and trained team members. Belbin suggests the following roles and descriptions which contribute to the performance of a team:

- *plant*: creative, imaginative, unorthodox, solves difficult problems;
- *resource investigator*: extrovert, communicative and enthusiastic, explores opportunities and develops contacts;
- *co-ordinator*: mature, confident and an effective chairperson, clarifies goals, promotes decision-making and delegates well;
- *shaper*: challenging, dynamic, thrives on pressure, has the drive and knowledge to overcome obstacles;
- *monitor/evaluator*: sober, strategic and discerning, sees all the options and judges accordingly;
- *teamworker*: co-operative, mild, perceptive and diplomatic, listens and avoids friction;
- *implementer*: disciplined and reliable, conservative and efficient, turns ideas into practical solutions;
- *completer*: conscientious, anxious, searches out errors and omissions and delivers on time;
- *specialist*: single-minded, self-starting, dedicated, provides knowledge and skills.

B

Although the above provides a list of positive role attributes, each also includes a number of allowable weaknesses. However, a mix of roles is needed for optimum group performance.

Belbin, M. (1993) *Team Roles at Work*, Oxford: Butterworth-Heinemann.

Beliefs

A belief is a description of the world around us, the things in it and the relationships within it. Beliefs are judgements, **evaluation**s or formed impressions which individuals make about themselves or the things around them. Beliefs are *generalisations* about things such as causality or the *meaning* of specific events; they are neither true nor untrue and therefore not facts. Beliefs not only affect how people behave but also what they pay attention to (or perceive). When people believe something is true, they are more likely to seek out information which supports that belief. Beliefs alter expectations. People perceive what they *expect* to perceive.

See **attitudes, attitude formation, values.**

Dilts, R. B. (1999) *Sleight of Mouth: The Magic of Conversational Belief Change*. Capitola, CA: Meta.

Below the line

'Below the line' and '**above the line**' are **marketing** terms. Below the line represents a number of **marketing** and **public relations** activities such as **promotion**s, **point of sale, direct mail, exhibitions, demonstrations**, etc.

Wilshurst, J. (1993) *Below-the-Line Promotion* (Marketing Series: Professional Development). London: Butterworth-Heinemann.

Benefits

Benefits refers to the positive contribution, assets or features of a product. They form part of the added value of a product and are highlighted in **marketing communications**.

Benn's Media Directory

Benn's Media Directory is one of the most detailed country-by-country sources for newspapers and magazines. Produced each year in three separate volumes, it covers the UK, Europe and the (rest of the) world. The directory is an important source of media contacts and information for the **public relations** practitioner and is vital for **media planning** and **media scanning**.

www.hollis-publishing.co.uk/benns

Bernays, Edward

Named as one of the hundred most influential Americans of the twentieth century by *Life Magazine*, Edward Louis Bernays (1891–1995) is considered the 'father of public relations', along with Ivy

B

Lee. Bernays was the nephew of the psychoanalyst Sigmund Freud and one of the first people to try to manipulate **public opinion** using the psychology of the subconscious. He was interested in the 'herd instinct' and the 'group mind' and considered it possible to control and regiment the masses without their knowledge. He called this scientific technique of opinion-moulding the 'engineering consent'. One of Bernay's favourite procedures for manipulating **public opinion** was the use of third-party **endorsement**s to plead his clients' causes. In order to promote the sales of bacon, for example, he conducted a survey of physicians and reported their recommendations that people eat a good breakfast. In his book, *Propaganda* (1928), Bernays argued that the manipulation of **public opinion** was a vital part of democracy.

Tye, L. (2002) *The Father of Spin: Edward L. Bernays and the Birth of Public Relations*. New York: Henry Holt.

Bernstein's wheel

Bernstein devised a wheel to illustrate the links between an organisation and its **publics** and the channels it uses to communicate **messages** to these **audience**s (see Figure 1). He suggested that every channel should be considered when an organisation wishes to communicate with its **publics**. His wheel indicates that the communicator has $9 \times 9 = 81$ combinations of both channel and **audience**. There are also 'intra-channel' options. The public relations channel, for example, includes within it numerous tactical combinations. Bernstein's wheel demonstrates the formidable array of options open to the **public relations** role.

Theaker, A. (2006) *The Public Relations Handbook*. Abingdon: Routledge.

B

BFD formula

Public relations practitioners must attempt to teach their **audience** on all three levels: intellectual, emotional and personal. The BFD formula stands for the emotions and aspirations which drive a prospective customer and are expressed as **Beliefs**, Feelings and Desires:

- What does the **audience** *believe*. What is their attitude towards the product or service?
- What does the **audience** *feel* about the major **issue**s in their lives, businesses or industries?

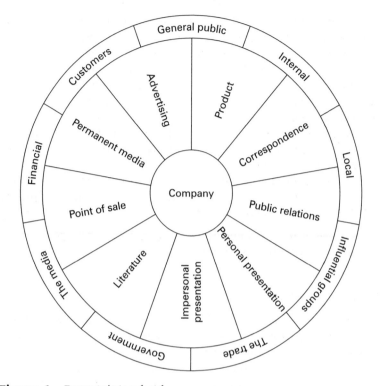

Figure 1   Bernstein's wheel
Source: Theaker (2006, 60). Used by permission of Continuum Publishers.

- What do the audience *desire*? What are their aspirations and goals? What change do they want in their lives that your product or service can give them?

See **AIDA model**.

Blog

A blog (a portmanteau of 'web' and 'log') has entries which are written in chronological order. It is similar to an on-line diary. Most blogs are primarily textual but may include images. Blogs have gained increasing notice and coverage for their role in breaking, shaping and **spin**ning news stories and are often used by politicians to voice opinions on international events. Blogs are used internally to enhance communications and culture in an organisation or externally for **public relations**, **advertising** or

marketing purposes – when they are termed 'corporate blogs'. There are different kinds of blogs:

- *vlog* – a blog comprising videos;
- *linklog* – a blog comprising links;
- *sketchblog* – a site containing a portfolio of sketches;
- *tumblelogs* – blogs with shorter posts and mixed media;
- *splog* – a blog used for the sole purpose of **spamming**;
- *slog* – a section or 'slice' of a regular business website, seamlessly integrated within the website structure but produced by blogging software.

One downside of the blog for **public relations** is that a disgruntled employee can post defamatory comments about the organisation. If not handled correctly, the organisation can find itself in a **crisis management** situation.

Barlow, A. (2007) *The Rise of the Blogosphere*. Westport, CT: Praeger.
Tremayne, M. (2007) *Blogging, Citizenship and the Future of Media*. New York: Routledge.

Boomerang effect

Understanding or being exposed to a message does not necessarily result in **persuasion**. Sometimes an advertisement is so annoying or plain silly that it has an effect which is the opposite of that which was intended. Instead of liking the product or the **message**, the respondent likes it less because the original **message** was so annoying. This is termed the 'boomerang effect'.

Boosterism

Boosterism is an American slang term describing the act of 'talking up' one's town or city. It is a term commonly used in tourism **promotion**.

Boundary spanning

The term 'boundary spanning' refers to the public relation's role of intelligence-gathering, the **analysis** and interpretation of the **macro** and **micro environment**. Information about the specifics of contextual factors such as economic and financial facts and intelligence about technological developments will be garnered by the **public relations** practitioner and used to support the **issues management process**. **Public relations** can contribute its

B

detailed knowledge of **publics** and other types of intelligence to ensure that the views and **attitudes** of the various **stakehold- ers** who hold the well-being of the organisation in their hands are taken into account.

See **environmental monitoring.**

BRAD

BRAD (British Rates and Data) is a resource which provides vital information for the UK media community. With more media entries than any other source and comprehensive **advertising**-related information on each one, BRAD is essential for anybody involved in planning, buying or **research**ing media. BRAD has around thirteen thousand media entries which detail **advertising** costs and circu- lation and **audience**-reach figures. The BRADnet system enables users to access data on-line via multiple search criteria.

www.brad.co.uk

Brainstorming

Brainstorming is a technique which seeks to improve group decision- making. It is based on the belief that under given conditions a group of people will solve a problem more creatively than individuals working alone. The presence of the group allows individuals to 'bounce ideas off each other' or gives individuals an opportunity to suggest half-formed ideas that other group members may turn into more practical suggestions. The purpose of brainstorming is to produce new, creative ideas. Members of brainstorming groups are required to follow four main rules of procedure:

1 They must avoid criticising other group members' ideas.
2 They must share any suggestions, no matter how bizarre.
3 They must offer as many comments as possible.
4 They must build on others' ideas to create new ideas of their own.

Electronic brainstorming requires participants to sit at their PCs. They enter their ideas into one window. Their ideas then appear in a second window along with the ideas of the other group mem- bers. Electronic brainstorming has proved to be more successful than face-to-face brainstorming as it allows individuals to glance at the contributions of others at any time without having their train of thought interrupted. The electronic environment may help to

B

trigger disinhibition, making members feel freer to express their wildest notions without being concerned about negative reactions.

Connelly, T. (1997) 'Electronic brainstorming: Science meets technology in the group meeting room', in S. Kiester (ed.) *Culture of the Internet*. Mahwah, NJ: Lawrence Erlbaum, 263–276.

Brand

A brand is a name, term, design or symbol which identifies and differentiates products. It means everything which surrounds a company's offerings from external communication to staff behaviour and **attitudes** and environmental and physical surroundings. Both **consumer public relations** and **marketing communications** are concerned with the way the value of a brand affects people's buying behaviours. In some cases, for example Virgin, Sony and Hoover, the company name is the brand. In other cases the product, such as Fairy Liquid, is well known, but the parent company, such as Unilever or Procter & Gamble, is less well known. Naomi Klein (2000) suggests that the role of branding has been changing in the last fifteen years, that the brand itself has increasingly become the product. For example, Nike has become about sport rather than about shoes, and Microsoft about communications rather than about software.

Al and Laura Ries (2002), in their controversial book, *The Fall of Advertising and the Rise of PR*, argue that a new brand cannot be launched with **advertising** because it has no credibility and suggest that new brands can be launched only with **public relations**. They also redefine **advertising**'s role as 'brand maintenance' and **public relations** as 'brand- building'.

There are important **issue**s to consider when brand-naming and these are shown in Table 1.

Baines, P. *et al.* (2004) *Public Relations, Contemporary Issues and Techniques*. Oxford: Elsevier Butterworth-Heinemann, 47.
Klein, N. (2000) 'Tyranny of the Brands, *New Statesman*, 24 Jan., 25–28.
Ries, A. and Ries, L. (2002) *The Fall of Advertising and the Rise of PR*. New York: HarperCollins.

B

Broadcast media

Broadcast media includes television, radio, **Teletext** and **Ceefax**. The broadcast media is extremely valuable in **public relations** terms as it enables **messages** to be communicated to a mass **audience**. These **messages** have instant impact but can be

Table 1 Considerations of brand-naming

Consideration	Reason	Example
Memorability	Customers more likely to use service if it is memorable. More likely to become part of their 'evoked set' of related products/services/companies. It is more likely to spark the interest of innovators and early adopting customers if it is memorable.	Asda (supermarket) Egg (internet banking) Freeserve (ISP) FCUK (retailing)
Image	The name might convey what the organisation is about. If it does, it is important to determine among multiple **publics** exactly what that impression is.	Rentokil Consignia (retailing) Iceland.co.uk (retailing)
Distinctiveness	The name may differentiate the company, brand or product from its competitors or it may convey a special property.	Post-it! (office supplies) Viagra (pharmaceuticals) Kodak (electronics)
Packaging	The labelling may be of particular importance to the **public relations** team because of the necessity to comply with particular regulations or because it can offer a competitive advantage if certain labelling is adopted.	The Body Shop (not-tested-on-animals claim) Iceland (GM-free food – without genetically modified material)

Source: Adapted from Baines *et al.* (2004).

B

difficult to retain, being transient in nature. Television and radio both have global **audiences**. Satellite communications and advanced technology have introduced new channels nationally and internationally in different forms. CNN, for example, is seen by viewers all over the world. In the UK alone, network television attracts up to 40 million viewers, more than 25 per cent greater than the combined total readership of all our national daily papers. Radio has advantages over television in the transmitting of **public relations messages** in that it is not confined to indoor **audiences**. Not only is it a more mobile medium it is also more responsive than television, being able to broadcast local announcements very quickly.

Teletext and **Ceefax** are essentially 'visual magazine' programmes covering a wide variety of topics and giving information that the viewer can call up at will. The advent of cable and satellite television in the UK is paving the way for more interactive programmes.

Brochures

Brochures are pamphlets or leaflet advertisements which form part of a company's corporate literature. As such they are an important **tool** of **public relations** and communicate important **messages** about an organisation to its **audiences** or **publics.** They should be written using plain language and be eye-catching in design, tone and appeal. Brochures are often distributed as **direct mail** or at **exhibitions** and trade events.

Budget

A budget is a method of estimating costs and subsequently controlling them. It identifies work to be done within the **public relations programme/plan** and enables a clear **critical path analysis**, **Gantt chart** or timetable to be produced. The three principal **public relations** costs are time, materials and expenses:

B

- Time represents the person hours involved in carrying out the **public relations objectives**.
- Materials consist of all the goods and **resources** which need to be purchased on the client's behalf. These can include everything from postage, stationery and displays to more expensive items such as corporate literature and interactive video equipment.

- Expenses are the costs of fares, taxis, hotels, hospitality, catering, transportation, etc.

In her book, *Planning and Managing Public Relations Campaigns* (2004), Anne **Gregory** outlines budget headings, as shown in Table 2.

Table 2   Budget headings

Human	Operating costs	Equipment
Staff salaries	Printing and production	Office furniture
Employment costs (e.g. NI, pensions, **benefits**)	Photography	Computer equipment and consumables
Overheads and expenses (e.g. heat, light, office space)	**Media relations**	
	Conferences Seminars	
	Sponsorship etc. Operating expenses (e.g. telephone, stationery, post)	

B

Smith (2002) suggests that budgets can be drawn up in two different ways – *scientific* (using objective formulae) and *heuristic* (more subjective, possibly trial and error):

1 *Scientific*
   - *Objective and **tactics*** is based on a review of the **objectives** and a summary of the **strategy** and subsequent **tactics** required to achieve them. It is sometimes called the 'ideal' or 'task' approach.
   - *Modelling* uses a variety of econometric and simulation **techniques** to model how various budget levels may affect performance.
   - *Payback period* is the time taken for an **integrated marketing communications** campaign to pay back the costs.

- *Profit optimisation* argues that the investment in **marketing communications** is continued as long as the marginal revenue exceeds the marginal cost (i.e. as long as every £1 invested returns more than £1).

2 *Heuristic*

- *Percentage of turnover* uses a simple calculation of a fixed percentage of either past or anticipated turnover.
- *Competitive parity* uses the competition and their relative spend as a measuring tool.
- *Affordable* is based on using all available monies after costs are deducted from required profits.
- *Arbitrary* is where senior management arbitrate between the different views of the **marketing** team.

Gregory, A. (2004) *Planning and Managing Public Relations Campaigns*, 2nd edn. London: Kogan Page.

Smith, P. R. (2002) *Marketing Communications: An Integrated Approach*, 3rd edn. London: Kogan Page.

Baines, P. *et al.* (2004) *Public Relations, Contemporary Issues and Techniques*. Oxford: Elsevier, Ch. 10 – Budgeting.

Business to business (B2B)

B2B **public relations** is where the end customer or user is another business. For example, a canvas supplier may be involved in **public relations** activities designed to attract the business of manufacturers of sails or tents; a chicken-feed supplier will target chicken farms. B2B **public relations** promotes products and services to other businesses using **tactics** other than direct sales. These can include **advertising, direct mail, exhibitions** and trade show support, **brand**ing and interactive services such as **website** design and search-engine optimisation.

Business to consumer (B2C)

B2C public relations is where the end customer or user is a consumer rather than a business (as in **business to business (B2B)** public relations). It is one of the most common forms of public relations and relies on the full scale of public relations tools and techniques to fulfil its objectives.

Business writing

Business writing includes all the formal written messages of an organisation and forms part of the **internal communications**

B

programme. Business writing includes such pubic relations' **tools** as **reports, proposals**, memos, minutes and notes.

Byliner

A byliner is a story signed and 'authored' by an officer of a particular organisation. In reality, the article or story is ghost-written by the **public relations** practitioner. One of the major advantage of byliners is that they position officers as experts and credible sources by inference.

See **credibility (intrinsic and extrinsic).**

B

Cc

Calendar listings

All newspapers and many other types of publications list details of forthcoming events for their readers. These calendar listings can provide a basic **public relations** tool if the organisation has an event which is open to the public and which they wish to advertise.

Call to action

The call to action is a **marketing** term for the part of any written or visual communication which encourages the prospect to buy the product or service by giving contact details, usually a **website** address, mailing address, telephone number or e-mail address.

Case studies

The profession of **public relations** relies heavily on case studies as a means of understanding itself through the condensed wisdom of the profession. Agencies keep case studies on file to preserve memories of **techniques** used and problems solved. Professional and scholarly journals publish cases which testify to the successes and failures of past **public relations programmes/plans**. Specialities such as **crisis management** and communications use case studies to legitimise practitioners' expertise. Artfully crafted case studies can become a valuable means of monitoring and improving education, theory and practice.**The Chartered Institute of Public Relations** in the UK bestows annual awards, the Pride Awards, on the basis of case studies that organisations submit.

Pauly and Hutchinson (2001) suggest that there are three uses of **public relations** cases:

- Campaign summary
  Goal: describe the steps involved in planning, implementing and evaluating a **public relations programme/plan**.
  Uses: show students how to assemble and conduct a

campaign. Record a department's or an agency's **public relations** activities for future reference. *Questions to ask*: what was the purpose of the campaign? What happened in this campaign and why?

- Case method
  Goal: teach **public relations** students to think strategically and critically.
  Uses: show students how a reflective practitioner solves the problem.
  Questions to ask: what would the student do under these circumstances?

- Case study (see **case studies**)
  Goal: analyse the theoretical significance of some set of **public relations** activities by placing them in historical, social, economic, political or ethical context.
  Uses: deepen knowledge of **public relations** as a communication practice.
  Questions to ask: why are these **public relations** activities worthy of study?

Pauly, J. and Hutchinson, L. (2001) 'Case studies and their use in public relations', in R. L., *Handbook of Public Relation*. Thousand Oaks, CA: Sage, Ch. 30.

Causes and charities

An organisation or individual will often sponsor a charity or a good cause as a mutual benefit and as part of their **corporate social responsibility** programme. This may be something as simple as donating a percentage of profits to a charitable cause or it may be sponsoring a local event or paying for **advertising** space in a local magazine. Alternatively, it may be on a larger scale; most larger corporations donate to national charities.

See **non-profit public relations, sponsorship.**

C

Celebrity spokespeople

Public relations practitioners often hire celebrities to act as **spokespeople** for an organisation. This celebrity **endorsement** is a successful method of attracting media support and attention and can add substance to a **public relations** story. Celebrity **endorsement** is most often used as part of an organisation's **corporate social responsibility** programme. Celebrities often offer their services free of charge to support a cause in which they have faith.

Redmond, S. and Holmes S. (eds) (2007) *Stardom and Celebrity: A Reader*. London: Sage.

Central Office of Information (COI)

The COI is the Government's centre for excellence for **marketing** and communications. The COI works with government departments and agencies to produce information campaigns on **issue**s which affect the lives of every citizen – from health and education to **bene-fits**, rights and welfare. The organisation combines expertise in **marketing communications** with an understanding of government systems and procurement policies. The COI's Chief Executive reports to the Minister for the Cabinet Office and the organisation is given annual ministerial targets to achieve.

www.coi.gov.uk

Change management

Change management is a structured approach to change in individuals, teams, organisations and societies which enables the transition from a current state to a desired future state. Each change in an organisation's infrastructure brings different opportunities and threats of which the **communication manager** should be aware. Change-management programmes, typically organised by human resource management departments, have a pivotal role to play during mergers, takeovers, the writing of **mission statement**s and value programmes and re**brand**ing/positioning initiatives. There is a strong role for **internal public relations** professionals during the management of any change. They have an important role to play in developing an understanding among employees of management expectations and vice versa during this time of reorganisation. A key component of change management is that it should not be concerned only with informing employees of what needs to be done but should also listen to their concerns about the impact any change will have on their work and lives.

Senior, B. (2006) *Organizational Change*, 3rd edn, Harlow: FT Prentice Hall.

C

Chartered Institute of Public Relations (CIPR)

The CIPR is the UK's leading **public relations** industry professional body. Founded in February 1948, it now has over eight thousand members. The CIPR is the largest association of its kind in Europe. It is a member of the European PR Federation and a founding member of the Global Alliance for Public Relations and Communications Management. The CIPR represents and serves the interests of people working in **public relations** in the UK and abroad and offers access to information, advice and support. It also provides **networking** and training opportunities through a wide range of events, **conferences** and workshops.

www.ipr.org.uk

Cheat sheets

As the majority of **journalist**s have a heavy workload, many appreciate **press packs** which present key information in an easily accessible format. Cheat sheets are short, bulleted information sheets which encapsulate the main points and a couple of angles within the main **press release**.

Client–consultant relationships

Client–consultant relationships are understood as those between an outside consultant and a client organisation. They are supported by a legal infrastructure contained in the **contract** and the agreed programme of work.

Clifford (Max)

Maxwell Frank Clifford is a highly controversial publicist practising the **press agentry** model of **public relations**. He runs Max Clifford Associates in Mayfair, London, representing well-known celebrities such as Simon Cowell and Big Brother winner Shilpa Shetty. As well as representing celebrities and people wishing to sell 'kiss and tell' stories to tabloid newspapers, Max campaigns tirelessly for the children's hospice at the Royal Marsden Hospital.

www.maxclifford.com

Closed questions

Closed questions ask for basic, limited and factual information. They can usually be answered with a short response selected from a limited number of possible options, often 'yes' or 'no'. Closed questions are used in fact-finding and data-gathering encounters for **research** purposes.

See **analysis, qualitative research methods, questionnaires, research**.

Closed system

See **open system**.

Code of Professional Conduct

The Code of Professional Conduct drawn up by the **Chartered Institute of Public Relations (CIPR)** sets down standards which make for good relationships and reputable business dealings by **public relations** practitioners. There are also other internationally adopted codes of conduct which have the support of the institute. The Code is binding to all members of the CIPR, is under constant review and is one of the most important documents for a **public relations** practitioner to digest. The following extract is sourced from www.ipr.org.uk.

CIPR Code of Professional Conduct
Introduction: Reputation is every organisation's most valuable asset. It has a direct and major impact on the corporate well-being of every organisation, be it a multinational, a charity, a Government Department or an SME. That is why the professionalism of those people who guard and mould reputation – PR professionals – is so important. As the PR profession continues to grow, the CIPR, as the voice of public relations practitioners, has an important role to play in ensuring that public trust and confidence is gained and guarded in the boardroom and on the high street alike.

Reliable and accurate information:
The CIPR operates a Code of Professional Conduct and disciplinary powers to which all members adhere. The Professional Practices Committee of the Institute handles complaints against members of the Institute who may be in breach of the Code.
The Code emphasises that honest and proper regard for the public interest; reliable and accurate information; and never misleading clients, employers and other professionals about the nature of representation or what can be competently delivered or achieved, are vital components of robust professional practice.

An evolving Code:
The Code is a living document which evolves to ensure that it keeps up to date. Following a consultation with members, it was reviewed and strengthened in March 2000. The resulting change incorporated areas such as CPD (continuous professional development) into the Code, and changed the Code into a document of best practice, in contrast with its previous 'thou shall not' approach.

C

In the years since, the Institute has grown both in size and stature. The award of the Royal Charter in particular made it important to beef up the Code, and to ensure that it was even more rigorous. Accordingly, and after consultation with members, the Code has been strengthened again.

The Code now allows the President or Director General to initiate an investigation against a member where substantive evidence of malpractice is brought to his attention, and where it is in the public interest to do so. This change means that we will no longer have to wait for a formal complaint before initiating the disciplinary procedure. It will allow us to enforce the high standards we expect with even greater rigour and authority. It is the next step of a maturing and increasingly self-confident profession.

Complaints against CIPR members:

The CIPR can investigate complaints made against only its members. If a PR practitioner is not a member, then they are not accountable.

All complaints remain confidential. Announcement of a complaint outcome is at the discretion of the Professional Practices Committee.

CIPR Code of Conduct
Section A
CIPR Principles

Members of the CIPR agree to:

1 Maintain the highest standards of professional endeavour, integrity, confidentiality, financial propriety and personal conduct;
2 Deal honestly and fairly in business with employers, employees, clients, fellow professionals, other professions and the public;
3 Respect the customs, practices and codes of clients, employers, colleagues, fellow professionals and other professions in all countries where they practise;
4 Take all reasonable care to ensure employment best practice including giving no cause for complaint of unfair discrimination on any grounds;
5 Work within the legal and regulatory frameworks affecting the practice of public relations in all countries where they practise;

6 Encourage professional training and development among members of the profession;

7 Respect and abide by this Code and related Notes of Guidance issued by the Institute of Public Relations and encourage others to do the same.

Principles of Good Practice:

Fundamental to good **public relations** practice are:

Integrity

Honest and responsible regard for the public interest;

Checking the reliability and accuracy of information before dissemination;

Never knowingly misleading clients, employers, employees, colleagues and fellow professionals about the nature of representation or what can be competently delivered and achieved;

Supporting the CIPR Principles by bringing to the attention of the CIPR examples of malpractice and unprofessional conduct.

Competence

Being aware of the limitations of professional competence: without limiting realistic scope for development, being willing to accept or delegate only that work for which practitioners are suitably skilled and experienced;

Where appropriate, collaborating on projects to ensure the necessary skill base;

Transparency and conflicts of interest;

Disclosing to employers, clients or potential clients any financial interest in a supplier being recommended or engaged;

Declaring conflicts of interest (or circumstances which may give rise to them) in writing to clients, potential clients and employers as soon as they arise;

Ensuring that services provided are costed and accounted for in a manner that conforms to accepted business practice and ethics.

Confidentiality

Safeguarding the confidences of present and former clients and employers;

Being careful to avoid using confidential and 'insider' information to the disadvantage or prejudice of clients and employers, or to self-advantage of any kind;

Not disclosing confidential information unless specific permission has been granted or the public interest is at stake or if required by law.

C

Maintaining professional standards

CIPR members are encouraged to spread awareness and pride in the public relations profession where practicable by, for example:

Identifying and closing professional skills gaps through the Institute's Continuous Professional Development programme;

Offering work experience to students interested in pursuing a career in **public relations**;

Participating in the work of the Institute through the committee structure, special interest and vocational groups, training and networking events;

Encouraging employees and colleagues to join and support the CIPR;

Displaying the CIPR designatory letters on business stationery;

Specifying a preference for CIPR applicants for staff positions advertised;

Evaluating the practice of public relations through use of the CIPR Research;

Evaluation Toolkit and other quality management and quality assurance systems (e.g. ISO standards); and constantly striving to improve the quality of business performance;

Sharing information on good practice with members and, equally, referring perceived examples of poor practice to the Institute.

www.cipr.org

Cognitive dissonance

Cognitive dissonance is a psychological term describing the uncomfortable tension which may result from having two conflicting thoughts at the same time or from engaging in behaviour which conflicts with one's **beliefs**. Simply, it can be the filtering of information which conflicts with what you already believe in an effort to ignore that information and reinforce your **beliefs**.

In **public relations** terms dissonance can take place after a purchase or 'buying into' an organisation's **message** when the purchaser is unsure about his/her decision and begins to question the wisdom of his/her purchase. In order to alleviate the dissonance, customers will rationalise their buying decision by changing cognitions and by concentrating on the positive aspects and ignoring the negative ones. A common **strategy** for dealing with dissonant **messages** is for **public relations** practitioners to attempt to change a consumer's **beliefs** about a product or service by communicating its **benefits**.

See **cognitive response model, persuasion, routes to persuasion.**

Festinger, L. (1970) *Theory of Cognitive Dissonance*, Stanford, CA: Stanford University Press.

Cognitive response model

The cognitive response model claims that **persuasion** occurs when the **audience** has thoughts or cognitions in response to a persuasive **message** and suggests that **audience** members can therefore be active participants in the **persuasion** process. Simply put, this means that **persuasion** is not in itself caused by **messages** but by the receiver's thoughts about these **messages**. In other words, if the receiver has thoughts which agree with the **message**, they are more likely to be persuaded by that **message**. This means that if **public relations** practitioners want to understand **persuasion**, they must first understand what receivers are likely to think about a **message**.

See **cognitive dissonance, persuasion, routes to persuasion.**

Communication audit

The communication audit is an extensive **research** tool which examines in detail the communication process itself. The audit identifies those **publics**, actual and potential, which are vital to an organisation's success and ensures that all those **publics** are reached. It critically examines the nature and quality of the communication **messages** which are being relayed and judges their effectiveness. It identifies any gaps in the communication process and recognises any potential opportunities which could be exploited. It will also consider channels of communication and any barriers to effective communication within the organisation. The audit is also proactive in that it looks ahead to identify future communication needs and pinpoints the skills and **resources** needed to implement an effective **public relations programme/plan**. The general goal of the audit is to identify how an organisation interacts with key **audiences**. Once the information is **research**ed, formal recommendations for preserving and enhancing the processes are presented.

The four-step audit process:

1 *Planning*: identify all **stakeholders** and decision makers. Draft a plan to interact with all **publics**.

C

2 *Audit*: gather information via **tools** such as surveys, **interviews, focus groups**, network **analysis, content analysis**, technology assessment, critical incident **analysis** and document **analysis**.

3 *Analysis*: evaluate and make recommendations based on the information found during the audit.

4 *Reporting*: create a formal document and present with professional recommendations to optimise communications.

See **publics, situation analysis.**

Communication manager

The communication manager plans and manages the **public relations programme/plan**, undertakes **research** and **evaluation**, counsels management and makes communication decisions.

See **communication technician, expert prescriber.**

Communication technician

The communication technician is not directly involved in making communication decisions, but carries out the **tactics** outlined within the **public relations programme/plan** such as writing **press release**s and **feature articles**, editing **house journals** and writing web pages. The communication technician is concerned with the implementation of the **public relations programme/plan** rather than understanding **research** or undertaking **evaluation**.

See **communication manager.**

Communication theory

In its simplest form, communication theory consists of transmitting information from one source to another and is best described by Harold **Lasswell**'s maxim: 'who says what to whom in what channel with what effect'. It is helpful to examine communication theory from one of the following viewpoints:

- *Mechanistic*: this view considers communication to be a perfect transition of a **message** from the sender to the receiver.
- *Psychological*: this view considers communication as the act of sending a **message** to a receiver and the thoughts and feelings of the receiver upon receiving and decoding the **message**.

- *Social Constructionist*: this view considers communication to be the product of the interactants sharing and creating meaning.
- *Systemic*: this view considers communication to be the new **messages** created via 'throughput' or what happens as the **message** is being interpreted as it travels through people.

A basic model of communication was devised by **Shannon and Weaver** in 1949 (Marsen, 2000). In Figure 2 the information source, which can be human or technological, produces a message which is transformed into a set of signals by a transmitter. These signals are sent out via a channel to a receiver, who decodes the **message**. The received **message** then reaches its destination. A noise element which is outside of the message can interfere with the sender's original intention which may cause failures in the communication.

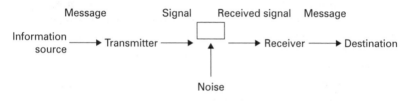
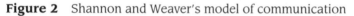

Figure 2   Shannon and Weaver's model of communication

If we were to apply **Shannon and Weaver**'s model to an instance of **public relations** communication, the information source would be the **public relations** practitioner, the **message** would be a news story, the channel would be a **news release**, the receiver would be a **journalist** and one possible example of 'noise' could be the fact that the **news release** was not newsworthy enough to warrant a **public relations** story.

See **Laswell, Osgood-Schramm's model of communication**.

Marsen, S. (2000) *Communication Studies*, Basingstoke: Palgrave Macmillan.

C

Community relations

Community relations describes the communications between a **public relations** professional (on behalf of an organisation) and the local community. The consideration of community relations is a vital part of the **public relations programme/plan** as an organisation's local community can influence the perception of the organisation's reputation. Community relations often forms part of the organisation's **corporate social responsibility plan.** The local community forms part of the organisation's overall **publics.**

See **activism, corporate social responsibility, publics.**

Competitions

The running of competitions in the local media is an inexpensive and accessible **tool** of **public relations** resulting in instant awareness of an organisation's existence.

Computer-mediated communication systems (CMCS)

CMCS is a method used by **public relations** professionals to reach the media first and so control the content and quality of **messages** considered essential to the maintenance of a positive **corporate image**. Corporations systematically develop **messages** which are designed to influence **stakeholders** and **opinion leaders.** These **messages** can be created through the development of **website**s to form user groups for **feedback** from **publics** and the use of **e-mail** to communicate more quickly with an organisation's **publics**. New communication technologies create alternative venues for individuals to develop computer-mediated communities and for **publics** to evolve. Electronic commerce, web pages and on-line advertisements tend to be the focus of CMCS for **public relations**. Consequently, the emergence of unregulated on-line social organisations has generated concerns over the possibility of a 'cyber**crisis**' in **public relations**.

Flew, T. (2005) *New Media: An Introduction*, 2nd edn. South Melbourne: Oxford University Press.

C

Conferences

Conferences are an excellent method of direct communication, with many opportunities for good **public relations**. Conferences generally fall into two categories – the **press conference** and the general conference. The general conference usually covers a variety of topics with a central theme and is a combination of plenary sessions, workshops, audio-visual displays and presentations and sometimes small trade **exhibitions.** Conferences can vary from the large and impersonal, for example a party political conference lasting five days, to the one-day affair with a number of set speakers.

Conferences lasting more than one day are often residential and require considerable planning and forethought.

Confidentiality

The **Code of Professional Conduct** of the **Chartered Institute of Public Relations (CIPR)** states that **public relations** practitioners should:

- safeguard the confidences of present and former clients and employers;
- be careful to avoid using confidential and 'insider' information to the disadvantage or prejudice of clients and employers, or to self-advantage of any kind;
- not disclose confidential information unless specific permission has been granted or the public interest is at stake or it required by law.

Conflict of interests

Public relations practitioners should be aware of any conflict of interests when dealing with clients. They should aim to be transparent in their dealings and:

- disclose to employers, clients or potential clients any financial interest in a supplier being recommended or engaged;
- declare conflicts of interest (or circumstances which may give rise to them) in writing to clients, potential clients and employers as soon as they arise;
- ensure that services provided are costed and accounted for in a manner which conforms to accepted business practice and **ethics**.

See **Chartered Institute of Public Relations (CIPR), ethics.**

C

Conflict resolution

Conflict among **stakeholders** and **publics** requires immediate attention and resolution in order to encourage organisational success. As a result, the field of conflict management strategies in **public relations** has become essential and is centred around **negotiation tactics**. The **benefits** of these **tactics** lie in the building of long-term relationships with strategic **publics** based on **two-way communication**, problem-solving, trust, **strategic**

planning and control mutuality. Conflict resolution in **public relations** evolved from **Grunig's four models of public relations**, the most sophisticated being the **two-way asymmetrical** and the **two-way symmetrical** models. The desired end result in **negotiation** is a **win–win** situation for all parties involved.

Buchanan, D. and Hucznski, A. (2004) *Organizational Behaviour: An Introductory Text*, 5th edn. Harlow: FT Prentice Hall, Ch. 23 – Conflict.

Congruity theory

Scholars Osgood and Tannenbaum addressed some of the problems of **balance theory**, by adding a measurement relating to the strength of the positive and negative **attitudes** found. Congruity theory is concerned about the gap between differing **attitudes** and how these parties can achieve congruency or a form of agreement. The theory postulates that there must be a measurement of adjustment of both attitude **evaluation**s until they come into alignment on a scale measured from plus three to minus three (see Figure 3). This adjustment must be equal to the total measure of the discrepancy. Stronger **attitudes** are often harder to adjust and so the **evaluation** which is rated furthest from the centre, (the nought figure) will be adjusted less. This theory is useful for **public relations** practitioners when considering **attitudes** to such **techniques** as **celebrity endorsements**, corporate **sponsorship** and other **public relations techniques** with possible ethical **issue**s.

See **balance theory.**

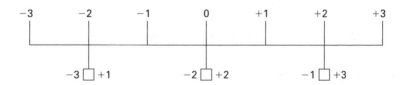

Figure 3 A scale for measuring attitude adjustment to achieve congruity (after Osgood and Tannenbaum)

Constraint recognition

Constraint recognition is the extent to which people believe that there are certain constraints which are preventing them from behaving in a particular way. If people perceive that there is a major problem, they are unlikely to seek more information. However, if they believe that there are few constraints on their behaviour they will seek out information from all sources. While constraint and **problem recognition** usually determine how much information a person wants about a situation, the level of involvement a person has with that situation will also affect how much they recognise a problem and will do something about it.

See **problem recognition.**

Consultancies

Public relations work is usually carried out **in-house** or by a **public relations** consultancy. The income of **public relations** consultancies comes from fees based on expertise, experience and the number of hours worked on a particular client's account. In the UK there are a number of **public relations** consultancies, ranging from those which are very large and internationally based to the smaller one-man bands. Some offer specialised consultancy services such as **media relations** while others offer a 'full service'. **Public relations** consultancies are normally employed for the following reasons:

1 The organisation is too small to justify having its own **public relations** department.
2 Company policy states that all **public relations** work must be handled externally.
3 The organisation requires specialist services such as **financial public relations** or **lobbying**.
4 The organisation requires expertise within a **media relations** programme.
5 Convenience – a consultancy can provide localised services such as **event management** for a national or international organisation.
6 The organisation requires a consultancy to manage a 'one-off' project.

Many consultancies in the UK are members of the **Public Relations Consultant's Association (PRCA)** which was established to raise and maintain professional and ethical standards in consultancy practice in the UK. For a consultancy to become eligible for membership of the PRCA, it has to pass the Consultancy Management Standard (CMS) assessment. This is a comprehensive assessment covering all areas of reputable business operation and reflecting the **objectives** of the PRCA's **mission statement**:

- to raise and maintain ethical and professional standards in consultancy practice;
- to provide facilities for government, public bodies and associations representing industry, trade and others to confer with **public relations** consultants as a body;
- to promote confidence in consultancy work and **public relations** as a whole and act as spokesmen for consultancy practice;
- to educate potential clients, establishing the reputation of professionalism of members who conform to the professional charter;
- to ensure that there is a professional practices committee to oversee standards and arbitrate on complaints;
- to offer practical industry-wide training and development services;
- to monitor and react to perception among key opinion leaders;
- to provide a forum on key **public relations** industry **issue**s;
- to demonstrate the effectiveness of good **public relations** in consultancy work;
- to increase the opportunities for members to develop new business;
- to improve co-operation with fellow **professional bodies in the UK** and worldwide;
- to help members improve their efficiency, understanding, skills, professionalism and **ethics**.

Advantages of using a consultancy:

- Consultancies can offer a range of independent advice services based on knowledge and professionalism.
- They are more objective as outsiders and can act as the 'eyes and ears' of the client's reputation.

Disadvantages of using a consultancy:

- There may sometimes be a lack of communication between client and consultancy.
- Clients will only get what they pay for – a consultancy may only offer a partial service based on the terms of the contract.
- A consultancy may not initially be familiar with the **organisational culture** of the client organisation.

www.prca.org.uk

Consumer profiles

Consumer profiles are intended to identify and quantify the habits and characteristics of certain groupings of customer. It is a **marketing strategy** aimed at working alongside and supporting **public relations**. Being a market segment methodology, it allows the matching of products and services by businesses and organisations to the market, thus progressing and manipulating the buying habits of the customers. Reliable data used to quantify customers' buying habits are harvested through both **qualitative research methods** and **quantitative research methods**.

Consumer public relations

Public relations in the field of consumer relations is often regarded as **marketing communications**. **Marketing** is the identification of consumers' needs and how to fulfil those needs profitably, and **public relations** plays its part in that process by managing **reputation**. Organisations which consider consumers as one of their main **publics** or **stakeholders** are likely to be relating to them as buyers of their products. Cutlip *et al.* (1985) list seven forms of assistance to the **marketing** function which **public relations** can perform:

1 publicising news and events related to the launching of new products or services;
2 promoting established products or services to the extent that they are newsworthy;
3 creating a favourable **image** of the 'company behind the product';
4 arranging for public appearances of **marketing spokespeople**;
5 **research**ing **public opinion** in market areas;
6 focusing news media attention on sales **conferences, exhibitions** and other **marketing** events;
7 assisting in programmes concerning **consumerism**.

Hendrix (1995) suggests that impact **objectives** for **consumer relations** programmes might include the following:

- increasing knowledge about the company's products;
- promoting a more favourable opinion about the company;
- stimulating greater participation in **consumer relations** programmes and encouraging more positive **feedback** from consumer groups.

C

He also suggests that output **objectives** might include:

- distributing more consumer publications;
- developing employee/customer seminars and meetings with important consumer groups.

Cutlip, S. M., Center, A. H. and Broom, G. M. (1985) *Effective Public Relations*, 6th edn. Englewood Cliffs, NJ: Prentice Hall.

Hendrix, J. A. (1995) *Public Relations Cases*, 3rd edn. Belmont, CA: Wadsworth.

Consumerism

In many critical contexts, consumerism is used to describe the tendency of people to identify strongly with the products or services they consume. A culture which is pervaded by consumerism is often referred to as a consumer culture. Many anti-consumerists believe that a modern consumer society is created by **public relations**, **marketing** and media influence, rather than arising from people's natural ideas regarding the kinds of things they need. There are also critics of consumerism, notably Anthony Giddens, who comment on the pervasive effects of the consumer culture. However, a more contemporary definition of consumerism relates to the fact that the modern consumer has rights which are often supported by non-governmental organisations and consumer groups. Consumerism demonstrates to business that the individual consumer can no longer be persuaded by mass communication and that he/she has become more discerning and therefore more powerful.

Aaker, D. (ed.) (1982) *Consumerism: Search for the Consumer Interest*. New York: Free Press.

Content analysis

C

Content analysis is a **quantitative** and systematic method of determining the content of **mass media**, **press clippings** about the client/organisation, publications produced by the **public relations** department, speeches given by members of the organisation or any other communication **messages**. Content analysis determines what the communication was about. It can be used to identify themes discussed in clippings and to determine whether coverage was negative, positive or neutral. It can be used to support **longitudinal research** and to suggest that certain topics have too much or too little coverage. According to Stempel *et al.* (2003), content analysis has five major stages:

1 *Select a unit for analysis.* Decide whether to examine entire **articles**, paragraphs or sentences.

2 *Construct categories*. Decide which themes, **evaluation**al dimensions or other units to measure. Categories should be defined by what the **public relations programme/plan** was designed to communicate.

3 *Sample content*. Not all **press clippings** or **articles** need to be examined. **Articles** may be selected randomly. Take one entire week or reconstruct a hypothetical week or month from a year-long period.

4 *Code the units of analysis*. Classify **articles** or number of column inches into the categories chosen.

5 *Analyse the results by computer or hand tabulation*.

See **media monitoring**.

Stempel, G. H. (1981) 'Content analysis', in G. H. Stempel and B. H. Westley (eds) *Research Methods in Mass Communication*. Englewood Cliffs, NJ: Prentice Hall, 119–131.

Stempel, G. H., Weaver, D. H. and Cleveland Wilhoit, G. (2003) *Mass Communication Research and Theory*. Needham Heights, MA: Allyn and Bacon.

Contracts

Contracts form one of the most common experiences in **public relations** work. There are different types of contract, depending on the subject, and the laws surrounding contracts are complicated. Ideally a contract should be in writing, but sometimes it is verbal. For an offer to be made there needs to be a definite intention to create a legal situation. If one side offers, then the other side must agree to accept that offer – or not. An acceptance must be unconditional but if the acceptance of the offer is conditional and introduces new and different conditions, then it becomes a revised offer, which then needs an acceptance.

Henslowe, P. (2003) *Public Relations: A Guide to the Basics*. London: Kogan Page, App. 3 – Model Client Agreement.

C

Controlled media

Controlled media are all types of media which are physically produced and delivered to the recipient by the sponsor and can include any object which carries a client's name or **message**. Sponsors are unfettered by creative or ideological restrictions imposed by third-party **gatekeeper**s such as news editors and entertainment producers. Controlled media allow sponsors to control the order of presentation and the integrity of the information provided. Unlike **interactive media**, controlled media communicators assume total responsibility for the design, production, manufacturing and distribution of **messages**. Controlled media also permit **messages** and communications to be targeted to particular **audience**s. The reader or viewer has direct access to unmediated **messages** such as the content of **brochures**, fact sheets or **direct mail.** In this way the **public relations objectives** need not be compromised – practitioners can write what they like and hand it directly to the person who wants to read it. The practitioner can select 'exposure' to the **message** as one of the **objectives**, expecting to affect the cognitions and behaviours of the reader if the message reaches an **active** or **aware public.**

Convergence model of communication

The convergence model of communication emphasises the cyclical nature of the process of communication. In 1981 Rogers and Kincaid (Heath, 2000) developed the 'convergence' model in which the participants in communication give and receive information and explore their understanding to such an extent that there is **mutual understanding** and further exchanges are unnecessary. The model is particularly useful for understanding one-to-one **interpersonal communication** where levels of interaction are high and understanding is easy to check, and in other forms of communication where **feedback** is easy to gain – such as one-to-one briefings.

Heath, R. L. (2000) *Handbook of Public Relations*. Thousand Oaks, CA: Sage.

Copy-editing

When a manuscript or any written material is finalised and written, it is then ready for copy- editing. Copy-editing is the process of reading and checking in detail the actual words written. The words will be edited for consistency, style, syntax, grammar, spelling, readability and adherence to the house style.

Copyright

Copyright is a set of exclusive rights which regulate the use of a particular creative work or expression of an idea or information. Copyright exists in a wide range of creative, intellectual or artistic forms. Copyright law only covers the form in which ideas have been manifested. It does not protect the actual idea, concept, fact, style or technique which may be represented by the copyrighted work.

Copywriter

A copywriter is someone who practises **copywriting**.

See **copywriting**.

Copywriting

Copywriting is the process of writing the words (copy) which sometimes go with the images which promote a business, person, opinion or idea. It can be plain text, a written speech or a radio or TV advertisement – or a variety of other media. The main purpose of writing **promotion**al copy is to persuade or **influence** the reader or listener to act – either to buy a certain product or to accept a certain idea or point of view. Alternatively, copy might be intended to dissuade a reader or viewer from a certain course of action or **belief**. Copywriting can include the following:

- body copy
- **slogans**, strap lines or taglines
- **headlines**
- **direct mail**
- **jingles**
- **web** and internet content
- television and radio commercial **scripts**
- **press release**s
- **white papers**
- **speeches**
- mail order catalogues
- billboards and posters
- postcards
- e-mail and letters
- other **advertising** media

A **copywriter** is a person who manipulates words/images and applies creative strategies within media. These strategies are balanced to integrate the principles of the **marketing mix** of a specific sector with a writing style which may be informative, persuasive, subliminal or a combination of all three. Through doing this the **copywriter** communicates product or service **benefits**.

Applegate, E. (2004) *Strategic Copywriting: How to Create Effective Advertising*. Oxford: Rowman and Littlefield.

Bly R. (2005) *The Copywriter's Handbook: A Step-by-Step Guide to Writing Copy that Sells*, 3rd edn. New York: Henry Holt.

Crompton A. (1999) *The Craft of Copywriting*, 2nd edn. London: Random House.

C

Core competencies of a public relations practitioner

The core competencies of a **public relations** practitioner are outlined in Figure 4.

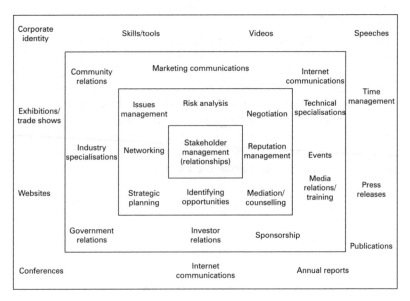

Figure 4   Core competencies of a public relations practitioner

Corporate apologia

Organisations today frequently find themselves the targets of criticism which challenges their legitimacy or social responsibility. It is against this backdrop that organisations respond to charges of wrongdoing with an apologia. This is not the same as an apology; rather it is an organisational response which seeks to present a compelling and competing account of its actions. Its motive is to 'clear its name' in order to protect its **corporate image** and manage its **reputation**. Benoit's theory of **image**-restoration strategies (1997) argued that when charged with wrongdoing, organisations and individuals seek to save face by using a combination of:

- denial
- responsibility evasion
- offensiveness reduction
- corrective action
- mortification.

A variant of denial is the use of the counter-attack in which organisations not only deny that they are guilty of any charges but also allege that their critics are suspected of having levelled false charges.

See **activism, crisis management.**

Benoit, W. L. (1997) 'Image repair discourse and crisis communications', *Public Relations Review*, 23, 177–186.

Corporate culture

Corporate culture consists of the **attitudes**, **beliefs**, experiences and **values** of an organisation. Sometimes known as 'the way we do things round here' (Hofstede 2001), corporate culture is made up of the specific collection of **values** and norms shared by people and groups in an organisation. Corporate culture controls the way they interact with each other and with **stakeholders** outside the organisation. Organisational **values** are **beliefs** about the kind of goals an organisation's members should possess and what behaviours they should show in order to bring about those shared goals. Organisational norms and expectations develop from these **values** and so bring about methods of controlling the behaviour of participating members. Strong culture exists where members respond to a stimulus because of their alignment with the corporate culture. Weak culture exists where members have little alignment to the corporate culture and where control must therefore be exercised through set procedures and bureaucracy. In order for **public relations** professionals to communicate clearly within and without the organisation, it is important for them to understand and recognise the concept of corporate culture. Several methods have been used to classify corporate culture. Some are outlined below.

Geert Hofstede identified five dimensions of culture in his study of national influences:

1 *Power distance*: the degree to which a society expects there to be differences in the levels of power.
2 *Uncertainty avoidance*: the extent to which a society accepts a level of uncertainty or **risk**.
3 *Individualism v. collectivism*: the extent to which an individual is expected to stand up for himself/herself versus the extent to which an individual will act as part of the group or organisation.
4 *Masculinity v. femininity*: the value put on traditionally male or female **values**, e.g. competitiveness v. collaboration.

5 *Long-term v. short-term orientation*: the importance attached by a society to the future versus that attached to the past and present. Thrift and perseverance are valued more by long-term societies while short-term societies value tradition and the reciprocation of favours.

Deal and Kennedy (1982) measured organisations in respect of **feedback** and **risk**. Using these **paradigm**s they suggested four classifications of corporate culture:

1 *The tough-guy macho culture*: **feedback** is rapid and rewards are high. This is often a stressful environment in which to work.
2 *The work hard/play hard culture*: this is characterised by few **risk**s being taken and rapid **feedback**. This is typical in large organisations which respect customer care and is often characterised by team meetings and jargon.
3 *The process culture*: this occurs in organisations where there is little or no **feedback**. Members become concerned with how things are done rather than with what is achieved and it is often associated with bureaucracies.
4 *The bet-your-company culture*: this is associated with slow feedback and reward but high risk. Stress results from high risk and delay, and the focus is on long-term preparation and planning. Typical examples may be pharmaceutical companies or oil-prospecting companies.

In 1985 Charles Handy explored a method of looking at culture which links **organisational structure** to corporate culture (Handy, 1993). He describes different cultures:

1 A *power culture* concentrates power among a few. Here the power radiates from the centre like a web. Power cultures have few rules and little bureaucracy.
2 In a *role culture* people have highly defined roles within a defined structure. Power derives from a person's position within the organisation. Typically these organisations form hierarchical bureaucracies.
3 By contrast, *task cultures* are teams formed to find solutions to particular problems. Power derives from expertise and these cultures often feature the multiple reporting lines of a matrix structure.
4 A *person culture* exists where all the individuals believe themselves to have equal power. Some professional partnerships often operate as person cultures.

C

Brown, A. (1998) *Organisational Culture*, 2nd edn. London: Pitman.

Deal, T. and Kennedy, A. (1982) *Corporate Culture: The Rites and Rituals of Corporate Life*. Reading, MA: Addison-Wesley.

Handy, C. (1993) *Understanding Organisations,* 4th edn. London: Penguin.

Hofstede, G. (2001) *Cultures Consequences, Comparing Values, Behaviours, Institutions and Organisations across Nations*, 2nd edn. Thousand Oaks, CA: Sage.

Corporate identity

Corporate identity is slightly different to **corporate image** in that it should be the same for all people, whereas **corporate image** may be relevant in different ways to different people. The creation and introduction of a corporate identity scheme can be a costly exercise and may involve some or all of the following:

- the livery of all forms of transport
- all stationery
- name displays
- **website**s
- **exhibition** stands and showrooms
- sales literature and **promotion**al material
- labels and packaging
- instruction leaflets
- uniforms
- corporate presents such as pens and key rings
- **point of sale** material
- advertisements
- credits on audio-visual material
- diaries and calendars
- **Annual Report**s and other communications for shareholders
- **hospitality** items such as crockery and cutlery etc.

Corporate identity schemes can have a consolidating effect with psychological results which can motivate and unite the workforce.

See **corporate image**.

Carter, D. E. (ed.) (2005) *Global Corporate Identity 2*. New York: Harper Design. www.wallyolins.com

C

Corporate image

A corporate image is a generally accepted concept for 'what the company stands for' – or how the organisation is perceived. It comprises all the visual, verbal and behavioural elements which make up the organisation and should accurately reflect the organisation's commitment to excellence, quality and relationships with its various **stakeholders**. Marketers and **public relations** professionals create a corporate image in order to suggest a mental picture to the public. Typically a corporate image sparks interest among consumers and generates **brand** equity based on the company's perceived **values**. Both product sales and reputation are enhanced by a carefully conceived corporate image. Consequently the corporate image is a major strategic concern which has a direct impact on the level of success which the organisation achieves through its **public relations** and **marketing** efforts. It is vital that the corporate image be consistent with the positioning of the organisation's product or core **message**. Any incongruency between the two will only confuse the organisation's **publics** and reduce sales or the impact of the **message**. The corporate name and **logo** should also be consistent with the overall corporate image. A weak or a strong corporate image can make a significant difference to the economic performance of an organisation, the acceptability of its products and services and even its human **resources**.

Marconi, J. (2000) *Image Marketing Using Public Perceptions to Attain Business Objectives*. Lincolnwood, IL: NTC Business Books.

Howard, S. (1998) *Corporate Image Management: A Marketing Discipline for the 21st Century*. Oxford: Butterworth-Heinemann.

Corporate social responsibility (CSR)

According to the **Chartered Institute of Public Relations (CIPR)**, CSR describes the role a company has in society. Cutlip *et al.* (1985, 393) state that 'an institution's relationships with its neighbours in its community are crucial because these neighbours supply the organisation's workforce, provide an environment that attracts or fails to attract talented personnel, set taxes, provide essential services and can, if angered, impose restraints on the institution or industry'.

Corporate social responsibility is the continuing commitment by business to behave ethically and contribute to economic developments while improving the quality of life of the workforce and their families as well as of the local community and society at large. In today's competitive global marketplace, companies must recognise responsibilities beyond their traditional and legal duties in order to gain competitive advantage and to secure a good reputation.

Cutlip *et al.* (1985, 405–406) list seven kinds of activity which can be used in corporate community involvement:

1 *The open house*: a tour of the facilities of an organisation, enabling large numbers of the community to visit the premises and instilling a renewed sense of pride in their workplace.
2 *Special events*: events such as special seminars linked to the company's products.
3 *Extended internal publication circulation*: with the addition of special community news to be circulated to the wider community.
4 *Volunteer activities*: encouraging and helping employees to volunteer in their local community.
5 *Local **advertising***: controlling and focusing the **message** for local media.
6 *Contribution of funds*: sponsoring or donating money to local organisations, whether in cash or in kind.
7 *News services*: tailoring information to the needs of local media.

See **stakeholder model.**

Cutlip, S. M., Center, A. H. and Broom, G. M. (1985) *Effective Public Relations*, 6th edn. Englewood Cliffs, NJ: Prentice Hall.
Corporate Citizenship Company (2002) 'Top tips to communicating social responsibility', found on www.ipr.org.uk/member/Prguides/CSR,

Counselling role

The counselling role is one of three roles of **public relations**, the others being the **technician**'s role and the manager's role. Organisational **public relations** personnel are in the best position to counsel management on their **strategic planning** and management decisions. Progressive **public relations** practitioners have often learned to synthesise their strategic communications planning with well-developed relationship-building skills imperative for the success with the **publics** targeted by the **public relations** function. Because they know how to build these relationships they are often called on to direct, counsel and advise other organisational leaders in that effort.

See **communication manager, communication technician.**

Creative diamond

Creativity expert Andy Green (2007) suggests that the creative diamond is a model which underpins what makes any individual or team creative. It consists of four quotients which make up the four points of a diamond (see Figure 5):

- *IQ (intelligence quotient)*: intelligent people can use their IQ skills to gather information and identify new and emerging **trends** and developments to help understand the **objectives** they face in their communications. IQ skills are engaged when **research**ing or working on factual stories.
- *EQ (emotional quotient)*: often it is the emotions rather than the facts which provide the reality of a situation. EQ skills can help establish the bigger picture of any situation. EQ enables the situation to be handled positively and helps to encourage openness and information-sharing to adapt to the needs of different **audience**s. EQ skills are engaged when working on human-interest stories.
- *VQ (vision quotient)*: vision is paramount to success – the more defined a goal is, the more likely it is to be achieved. Creative **public relations** practitioners have a vision of a potential positive outcome to their communications challenge which is fuelled by positive thinking. Creative **public relations** thinkers use their vision to think beyond any immediate and short-term boundaries or problems. VQ skills are engaged when working on new and innovative campaigns.
- *AQ (adversity quotient)*: this relates to the level of willpower needed to keep going even when problems keep arising.

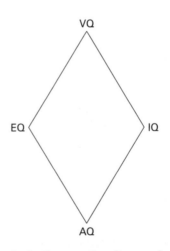

Figure 5   The four Qs in the creative diamond

AQ skills consist of resilience and flexibility and allow for a positive response to changes and challenges. AQ skills are engaged in **crisis** situations.

See **creativity (in public relations).**

Green, A. (2007) *Creativity in Public Relations*, 3rd edn. London: Kogan Page.

Creativity (in public relations)

Public relations work creates or manages change and therefore, according to creativity practitioner Andy Green, a working definition of creativity in **public relations** must contain some form of process and end product. He defines creativity as

> the ability each of us has to create something new by bringing together two or more different elements in a new context, in order to provide added value to a task. A creative act consists of not only originating but also evaluating the added value it contributes. It is not novelty for its own sake, but it must produce some sort of value that can be recognised by a third party . . . by introducing the creative dimension, practitioners must produce a new synergy to provide added value.

Green, A. (2007) *Creativity in Public Relations*, 3rd edn. London: Kogan Page.

Credibility (intrinsic and extrinsic)

Credibility refers to the perceptions of the source held by the receiver. When the source is perceived to be an expert in his/her field, credibility is high for the receiver. The source's prior **reputation** as credible also affects the **message**. This type of credibility is termed *extrinsic* because it is outside of the message itself. If the content of the message is perceived as silly or unfavourable, credibility is termed *intrinsic* because it comes from the receiver's reaction to the message itself. In other words it is created by the message. The distinction between the two forms of credibility is important for **public relations** practitioners because extrinsic credibility is a more reliable influence on **persuasion**. Consequently it is of vital importance for the sender of the message (the organisation) to have a solid and favourable reputation.

See **byliner, cognitive dissonance, cognitive response model, persuasion, routes to persuasion.**

C

Creolisation

Public relations management is an applied discipline which draws on sociology, psychology and other disciplines for its ideas. Creole is a term which emerged to describe language which resulted from the interrelations between two languages from two communities, usually one European language and the other from a colonising power. Subsequently, creolisation has become a process which draws on knowledge from disciplines with mixed boundaries – practice, academia, consultancy and the media. Processes of creolisation are apparent in **public relations** in the fact that the first generations of academics have in some cases gained graduate and postgraduate education in other disciplines and consequently bring a variety of insights to **public relations**.

Crisis

A crisis is an event (or events) which has possibly serious detrimental effects for an organisation. Regester and Larkin (2005) define a crisis as

> an event which causes the company to become the subject of widespread, potentially unfavourable, attention from the international and national media and other groups such as customers, shareholders, employees and their families, politicians, trade unionists and environmental **pressure groups** who, for one reason or another, have a vested interest in the activities of the organization.

Crises come in all shapes and sizes and can range from major crises such as aeroplane and ferry disasters to product-related crises. **Research** conducted in the 1990s by Business Planning and Research found the following crises most likely to occur:

- environmental pollution, hurricanes and floods
- product defects
- unwanted takeover bids
- sabotage
- the death of senior management members
- the kidnap of senior management members
- computer failure
- industrial disputes
- fraud and other financial crises
- fire and accidents

- **pressure groups** and **activism**
- sexual harassment.

See **crisis by criticism, crisis management, risk.**

Regester, M. and Larkin, J. (2005) *Risk Issues and Crisis Management: A Casebook of Best Practice*, 3rd edn. London: Kogan Page.

Crisis by criticism

Many companies and organisations have received negative media coverage as a result of prosecutions under the Trade Descriptions Act, Consumer Protection Act and various labelling laws. These offending **issue**s are widely published in the media. Investigative journalism can be very damaging to an organisation's **reputation** and the **public relations** practitioners finds themselves in a position of **crisis management**.

See **crisis, crisis management, risk.**

Crisis management

Crisis management is the reactive response to an organisational crisis. A **crisis** is an event or situation which causes the organisation to become the subject of widespread, potentially unfavourable attention from the local, national or international media. Unfavourable attention can also come from other groups such as shareholders, customers, employees and their families, politicians, trade unions and environmental **pressure groups** who for one reason or another have a vested interest in the activities of the organisation. If mishandled or mismanaged, a **crisis** can have a potentially devastating effect on the organisation, ruining its **reputation** and rendering it unviable. Changes in the marketplace, **issue**s with competitors and political, environmental, economic, social and technological changes are all situations which can exacerbate a **crisis**. A **crisis** generally occurs because potentially damaging **issue**s have not been previously identified by means of a competent **issues management programme**.

Any **crisis** response plan should include the following details:

- an assessment of the organisation's vulnerabilities;
- organisational background information to be provided to the media;
- an official statement from the chief executive officer;
- provision for a **crisis** information centre, interview areas and information management teams;

C

- prepared, fill-in-the-blanks **news release**s for the media, the public and the employees;
- contact details for all key personnel, plus a company-wide telephone list and e-mail addresses;
- provisions for media access and escorts.

Any **news release**s (or **press release**s) should follow the guidelines below:

- Gauge the amount of interest your **crisis** is likely to attract.
- Use bulleted points when writing the facts.
- Release all information on official letterheads.
- Put the date and time at the top of every page.
- Include the contact details of a person who can be contacted 24 hours a day.
- Double-space the information.
- Consult with legal counsel before releasing information.

Any negative reporting should be headed off thus:

- Disclose the facts of the story quickly and accurately.
- Provide updates as new information becomes available.
- Apologise but do not accept responsibility without consulting legal counsel.
- Demonstrate compassion for any victims.
- Review your organisation's **website** and remove any information which might be inappropriate during the **crisis**.
- Prepare **press packs** which put the **crisis** into context.
- Keep a log of what information is released, when and to whom.
- Never say 'no comment' – this will only fuel rumour and speculation.

See **crisis, crisis by criticism, risk.**

Regester, M. and Larkin, J. (2005) *Risk Issues and Crisis Management*: *A Casebook of Best Practice*, 3rd edn. London: Kogan Page.
Smith, D. and Elliott, D. (eds) (2006) *Key Readings in Crisis Management: Systems and Structures for Prevention and Recovery*. Routledge: London.

Critical discourse analysis

Critical discourse analysis is an interdisciplinary approach to the study of discourse, which views language as a constructed form of social practice. It focuses on the way in which text and talk produces social and political domination. Critical discourse analysis rests on the idea that access to linguistic and social **resources** is unequal and that **resources** are controlled institutionally.

The patterns of access to discourse and communicative occurrences are therefore necessary elements for critical discourse analysis. By implication, therefore, the use of **rhetoric** in **public relations** writing is necessarily sensitive to **issues** of social, economic, ethnic and sexual difference to asymmetrical relations of power which challenge or sustain those differences and to the **messages** which naturalise knowledge and truth.

Caldas-Coulthard, C. R. and Coulthard, M. (eds) (1996) *Texts and Practices: Readings in Critical Discourse Analysis*. London: Routledge.

Critical path analysis

A critical path analysis is similar to a **timetable** or a **Gantt chart** in that it identifies those elements of a **public relations programme/ plan** which involve the greatest amount of time. They are plotted on a chart – either vertical or horizontal – which demonstrates when each job in the programme will start and finish. Critical path analyses can be applied for single assignments such as the organisation and management of a **press release** or for annual plans, in which case the critical path will run from 1 January to 31 December. A critical path analysis is a fundamental part of campaign planning.

See **Gantt chart.**

Critical theory and critical thinking

Critical theory focuses on power and its distribution. It also explores the structures and processes which can limit human potential. Critical thinking has its basis in 1920s Western Marxism, which highlighted the unfair aspects of distribution and sought to change society. Critical thinking analyses arguments and aims to 'unpack' or 'unpick' concepts. It looks at both sides of an argument to test its validity. Cottrell (2005) suggested that critical thinking demands:

- a healthy scepticism;
- the patience to work through the arguments of others;
- open-mindedness;
- a need to be careful of personal emotional responses such as anger and frustration;
- the juggling of a range of ideas for comparison purposes;
- the need to support arguments with evidence and experience from 'real world' examples.

Critical thinking is particularly important in **public relations**, notably when **research**ing, planning and counselling.

Cottrell, S. (2005) *Critical Thinking Skills*. Basingstoke: Palgrave Macmillan.
Geuss, R. (1981) *The Idea of a Critical Theory: Habermas & the Frankfurt School*. Cambridge: Cambridge University Press, 1981

Cyber suspense

An element of surprise is needed in order to keep people coming back to the organisation's **website**. Matt Haig (2000) calls this 'cyber suspense' and suggests the following ways to turn the organisation's **website** into the on-line equivalent of a page-turner:

- Have a 'What's New' section. This will update visitors regularly to anything new in which the organisation is involved.
- Put a soap opera on the site. On some sites visitors can even watch developments in real time via a webcam.
- Order information in a series. Rather than revealing everything at once, any information should be given away in stages.
- Put a small amount of text on the home page as a teaser. Put large amounts of information at least two links away.

See **cyberspace public relations (e-pr)**.

Haig, M. (2000) *e-PR: The Essential Guide to Online Public Relations*. London: Kogan Page.

Cyberspace public relations (e-pr)

One of the greatest challenges facing public relations practitioners today will be in understanding and utilising the new communication technologies, which are being developed at a staggering rate. New technology is at the forefront of assembling, collecting and disseminating information in **public relations**. More information can flow more quickly to a global **audience** than ever before. A vast array of information on topics relevant to the content and process of **public relations** is available via **databases** and electronic news. One type of database which an organisation can employ in its own **public relations** efforts is its own **website** where information about the organisation and its **issue**s and **marketing** position can be accessed by interested parties 24 hours a day, 7 days a week. Cyberspace **public relations** also includes the ability to **research** on-line through the use of **surveys** and **interviews**. The internet allows for a type of speed and narrowness of information flow which is unparalleled and is especially useful for **issues management**.

Heath, R. L. (ed.) (2001) 'Cyberspace', in *Handbook of Public Relations*. Thousand Oaks, CA: Sage, Section 4 – Public Relations.

Dd

Data protection

Data protection is a term related to the storing of customer information or other personal details on a **database**. Data protection intends to protect individuals from the misuse of data stored by business or specialist data capturers. In most cases individuals have the right to access data stored about them and may seek redress if any information is found to be incorrect or misrepresentative. Data protection also protects the individual from indiscriminate sharing of stored data for **marketing** purposes.

Carey, P. (1998) *Blackstone's Guide to the Data Protection Act 1998* (Blackstone's Guides). London: Blackstone Press.

Databases

One of the most important advances offered by new technologies has been the development of databases. The size and content allows for a vast array of information on topics relevant to the content and process of **public relations**. Users can add to databases as well as using their content to understand an **issue** or to segment markets, **audience**s or **publics.** Databases include on-line newspaper copy and other forms of electronic news. One type of database which an organisation can employ in its **public relations** effort is its own web page. The use of databases also allows for **two-way symmetrical communication** and can thus be regarded as an important communication **tool**.

Defamation

In law, defamation is the communication of a statement which makes a false claim, expressly stated or implied to be factual, which may harm the reputation of an individual, business, product, group, government or nation. **Slander** is a transitory harmful statement, in the form of speech, gestures or sign language, while

libel is a harmful statement in a fixed medium, such as writing, pictures, signs or electronic broadcasts, including CDs, **DVDs** and **blog**ging.

If a statement is considered derogatory, there are still some circumstances in which it may be allowed, such as proving it to be the 'truth'. Proving adverse public character statements to be true is the best defence against prosecution for **libel**. 'Absolute privilege' means that a statement cannot be sued as defamatory, even if it were made maliciously; such as applies, for example, to evidence given in court. 'Qualified privilege' may be used as a defence by a **journalist** who believes the information, for example local government documents, to be in the public interest.

See **libel, slander.**

Demographics

Demographics involves the study of the human population and is generally considered a **marketing** term. Demographics measure a number of variables, including size, age, gender, density, location, race, occupation, income, mobility, marital status and educational attainment. The distribution of **values** within a demographic variable and across households are of interest to communicators, as well as trends over time.

See **psychographics, segmentation.**

Deontological reasoning

Broadly speaking, ethical thought and reasoning can be divided into **teleological** and **deontological** approaches. Ethical actions are those thought to result in the greatest good. Deontologists believe that good consequences are not in themselves sufficient to guarantee good actions. They believe that some acts must be done regardless of their consequences. Critics note, however, that sometimes correct actions can have bad consequences, for example when telling the truth will destroy another person.

See **ethics, teleological reasoning, utilitarianism.**

Designers

Designers and design **consultancies** specialise in particular areas of design work which enhance the work of the public relations

D

practitioner. Much design work today is computer- generated, which can be both effective and time-saving. When commissioning design work, the brief should always contain the following:

- clear aims and **objectives;**
- background information on the organisation or client;
- any existing work or house style which may help the design process;
- any constraints in operation, e.g. existing corporate colours, **logo**, typeface;
- target **audience**s;
- **values;**
- useful contacts;
- a **budget**;
- a **timetable.**

Once the roughs or initial ideas have been approved, the designer will produce final **proofs** for approval and finally the finished artwork.

Dialogic communication

Dialogic communication is a **two-way symmetrical** approach which facilitates collaborative processes and results in relationship-building. It is also referred to as diachronic communication.

Direct mail

Direct mail differs from **advertising** in that it attempts to send its **messages** directly to the consumer or other interested parties without mediation via unsolicited commercial communication. Marketers use a reduced rate 'bulk mail' postal rate to send paper communications to all postal customers in a given area or to all customers whose names and addresses have been taken from a given list. Direct mail comes in all shapes and sizes and some of the most common formats include:

D

- *catalogues*: multi-page, bound **promotion**s, usually featuring a selection of products for sale;
- *self-mailers*: pieces created from a single sheet which is folded in half or quarters;
- *poly-bag packages*: large, full-colour packages sealed in a clear plastic outer wrap for maximum impact;
- *postcards*: simple, two-sided pieces with a **promotion**al **message** on one side and the customer's address on the other;

- *envelope mailers*: mailings in which the **promotion**al material is placed within the envelope (this enables the marketer to include more than one insert);
- *snap mailers*: mailers which fold and seal with pressure;
- *dimensional mailers*: mailers which have some dimension to them, such as small boxes;
- *intelligent documents*: programmable mail pieces built from database information and printed digitally.

The use of direct mail as a **promotion**al tool has both advantages and disadvantages. It can be used directly to target the most likely purchasers and allow for statistical **analysis**. However, it is also a costly exercise. Large quantities of paper are wasted and there is always a danger of alienating potential customers if they feel communication is being forced upon them.

Discourse analysis

Discourse analysis is a general term for analysing written, spoken and signed language. **Critical discourse analysis** is an interdisciplinary approach to the study of discourse which focuses on the ways in which social and political domination is reproduced by text and language. Discourses are framed within narratives of one kind or another, for example within news narratives or **advertising** language. They operate to uphold particular interpretations of social life and can therefore be seen to be underpinned by ideologies and the power differences articulated within them.

See **ideology**.

Brown, G. and Yule, G. (1983) *Discourse Analysis*. Cambridge: Cambridge University Press. Fairclough, N. (1995) *Critical Discourse Analysis*. Harlow: Longman.

D

Dominant coalition

Organisations have many goals and these can change as the environment changes or when the organisation becomes involved in the process of **change management.** Organisations are made up of several constituencies – both internal and external. The internal constituencies are the individuals and departments which form the organisation, while the external constituencies may be other organisations which buy, sell or use the organisation's products or services – the government, consumers or **publics.** Each of these constituencies has a say in determining the organisation's goals, but the constituencies with the most power both inside and outside the organisation make up the dominant coalition of the organisation. In order to be effective, **public relations** professionals need to be part of that dominant coalition and so be at the forefront of any decision-making and goal-setting.

Dominant paradigm

The dominant paradigm in a field of work comprises those ideas and methodologies which guide the majority of the **research** in the discipline and are regarded as the most important ideas. Within **public relations**, the dominant paradigm is that which is the most popular or the majority approach to the subject. These ideas then become embedded into a formal set of ideas of what the discipline stands for.

See **paradigm.**

Domino theory of communication

In the late 1950s, work in the field of communications suggested that individuals sought information which agreed with their **attitudes** and resisted **messages** which conflicted with them. More recently, scholars have suggested that individuals select information because it has some relevance to them and not just because it reinforces their current views; in other words, receivers have become less passive and more active in seeking and receiving information so that they

D

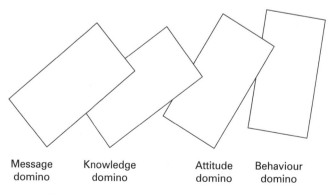

Message domino   Knowledge domino   Attitude domino   Behaviour domino

Figure 6   Effects of domino theory
Source: Adapted from Gregory (2004).

can exploit it to the full. This model of communication represents the knock-on effects of a falling domino – the **message** is received and this affects knowledge, which in turn affects **attitude,** which in turn affects behaviours (see Figure 6). The domino theory of communication is reflected in the **AIDA model**.

Gregory, A. (2004) *Planning and Managing Public Relations Campaigns*, 2nd edn. London: Kogan Page.

DVDs

A DVD is a D̲igital V̲ersatile D̲isc or D̲igital V̲ideo D̲isc. DVDs are popular optical disc storage formats and can be used as **promotional tools** in **public relations**.

Dyadic communication

Dyadic communication is communication which takes place on an interpersonal level between a representative of an organisation and an individual member of the public. One-on-one communications require excellent **interpersonal communication skills** but are often unstructured and unplanned. Examples of dyadic communications within a **public relations** setting include face-to-face solicitations of major donors by fund-raisers, responses to customer complaints, **lobbying** of law-makers, conflict **negotiation**s, counselling and bargaining.

D

Editorial

An editorial is an **article** in a magazine or newspaper which expresses the opinion of the editor, the **editorial board** or the publisher. An op-ed, or opposite editorial, is similar in content to an editorial but represents the opinion of an individual contributor who is often, but not always, associated with the particular publication. Editorials are often marked up separately in a column to indicate that they are different from ordinary news items and they often address current and/or controversial topics of public interest. Generally, editorials fall into four categories: news, policy, social and special. The editorial pages of a newspaper are about views rather than news and often take the form of a short essay or thesis, using argument to promote a certain point of view and follow a simple format:

1 Introduction
2 Statement of position
3 Reason 1 to support position
4 Reason 2 to support position
5 Reason 3 to support position
6 Acknowledgment of opponent's reasons and rebuttal
7 Summary, restatement of position and **call to action**.

Editorials of argument and **persuasion** take a firm stand on a problem or condition. They attempt to persuade the reader to think the same way. The editorial often proposes a solution or advises taking some definite action.

Editorials of information and interpretation attempt to explain the meaning or significance of a situation or news event. There is a wide variety of editorials in this category, ranging from those which provide background information to those which identify **issue**s. Editorials of tribute, appreciation or commendation praise a person or an activity. Editorials of entertainment have two categories: one is the short, humorous treatment of a light topic; the other is a slightly satirical treatment of a serious subject.

Editorial board

The editorial board consists of a group of editors who decide the tone and direction that the publication's **editorial**s will take.

See **editorial**.

Elaboration likelihood model

In 1980 Richard E. Petty and John T. Cacioppo created the elaboration likelihood model to explain how **messages** used **persuasion** in order to change the attitude of the receiver. They suggested that a message was transmitted and received through two routes of **persuasion**:

1 the central route
2 the peripheral route.

The central route claims that individuals are more likely to be persuaded by a message if they are able to think about and elaborate extensively upon that message – they are motivated by it. The peripheral route claims that if individuals are unable to elaborate extensively on the message then they may be still be persuaded by the actual content of the message itself. In other words they would be drawn to the message by positive factors with which they are already familiar. However this may only be a temporary attitude shift. A message must be persuasive if it is to be effective. A neutral message is a waste of time for both the sender and the receiver. A message should also have relevance to the receivers in order for them to be motivated to process on to the next step of **persuasion**. Once relevance is established, the receiver must have the ability to process, i.e. the message should be simple enough to allow for this. If the message is a strong one, it is likely that the receiver's behaviour can be predicted as a result of **persuasion**. However, if the message involves false information, the receiver will reject it, resulting in a **boomerang effect**. If the receiver is not motivated by the message or unable to process it, the message follows the peripheral route. Here the message will try to persuade the receiver by concentrating on an **issue** with which the receiver is already familiar, such as (in **advertising**) sex, money or celebrity. For example a celebrity may be used to sell a product and the receiver of the message buys the product purely because he/she likes and trusts the celebrity. Robert Cialdini identified six types of peripheral clues:

1 *Reciprocation* is the idea that the receiver is obliged to agree with the message because of some past experience or information.

2 *Consistency* means relying on thoughts held in the past, e.g. 'I liked it then, so I'll like it now.'

3 *Social proof* is similar to peer pressure. The actions and words of others are likely to influence a receiver of a new message.

4 *Liking* means simply that the speaker of the message is likeable in some way.

5 *Authority* is the sense that the speaker has some power over the receiver, perhaps because he/she is an expert on the **issue**.

6 *Scarcity* is the notion that the message will only be available for a limited time and that the receiver should act quickly.

Cialdini, R. B. (1993) *Influence: Science and Practice*. New York: HarperCollinsCollegePublishers.

Petty, R. E., Cacioppo, J. T. and Schumann, D. (1983) 'Central and peripheral routes to advertising effectiveness: The moderating role of involvement', in *Journal of Consumer Research*, 10 (Sept.), 135–146.

Electronic press packs

The trend towards electronic press packs is growing. Organisations are increasingly sending them electronically and posting them on their **website**s as a PDF file or as a word-processed file. Electronic press packs contain all the traditional inserts of a normal **press pack** but also include downloadable **image**s.

See **press packs.**

Employee communications

See **internal communications.**

Endorsement

See **testimonial.**

E

Entertainment sponsorship

The Broadcasting Act (1990) brought about huge changes in commercial **sponsorship** opportunities in UK broadcasting. The Independent Television Commission (ITC) replaced the Independent Broadcasting Authority (covering both independent television and radio) with responsibility for awarding regional commercial TV franchises, and the Radio Authority with responsibility for awarding both local and national commercial radio franchises. Under the act, commercial TV and radio programmes may now be sponsored, although the sponsor has no control over the programme and their products cannot be featured (see **product placement**). In the case of ITC programmes, there may be brief commercials in trailers, at the beginning and at the end of programmes. Probably the most well-known example of entertainment **sponsorship** is Cadbury's **sponsorship** of *Coronation Street*. Commercial radio **sponsorship**s take a slightly different form. Here the presenter will introduce the programme, stating that it is broadcast 'in association with' a sponsor, followed by a brief **strapline** or **slogan**.

See **properties and product placement, sponsorship.**

Environmental monitoring

Environmental monitoring, also known as environmental scanning or **boundary spanning** and **issues management** is **research** to detect **trends** in **public opinion** and in the socio-political climate of the organisation. It forms an important part of the **research** and **analysis** segment of the **public relations plan** and is swiftly followed by social auditing which determines the consequences for the **publics** of the organisation and the extent to which the organisation needs to correct these consequences.

The major **objectives** of environmental monitoring are to:

- detect political, economic, social and technological trends and changes in the marketplace;
- identify potential threats and opportunities for changes implied by those trends;
- promote forward-thinking and proactive management;
- compete in the market-place.

See **boundary spanning, issues management, PEST analysis, SWOT analysis.**

Morrison, J. L. (1992) 'Environmental scanning', in M. A. Whitely, J. D. Porter and R. H. Fenske (eds) *A Primer for New Institutional Researchers*, Tallahassee, FL: Association for Institutional Research, 86–99.

EPISTLE

EPISTLE is an expanded version of the **PEST analysis**. Here, as well as the four elements of PEST, separate consideration is given to Information, the Legal (or regulatory) aspects and the physical (or green) Environment.

See **PEST analysis.**

Ethics

The word 'ethics' is derived from the Greek *ethos* meaning 'customs'. Ethics is a major branch of philosophy, exploring right conduct and good living. It is far broader than basic concepts of right and wrong. Society operates around a given set of social or moral rules which guide human conduct. In the field of **public relations**, ethics is particularly important when considering **issues** of **corporate social responsibility**. Here business ethics focuses on how individuals use traditional ethical views to examine how organisations manage human behaviour. Recognition of the importance of ethical practice is also a major part of the **Code of Professional Conduct** of the **Chartered Institute of Public Relations (CIPR)**.

See **deontological reasoning, utilitarianism**.

Brenkert, G. G. (2008) *Marketing Ethics*. Oxford: Blackwell.
Fitzpatrick, K. and Bronstein, C. (eds) (2006) *Ethics in Public Relations: Responsible Advocacy*. Thousand Oaks, CA: Sage.

Euprera (European Public Relations Education and Research Association)

Euprera brings together academics and practitioners from across Europe and beyond to discuss shared **research** interests and develop practical and theoretical understandings of the communications discipline.

www.euprera.org

Evaluation

Evaluation is an ongoing process of review in order to determine the effectiveness of the **public relations programme/plan**. Practitioners will regularly evaluate the **media relations** element of the programme by making a critical **analysis** of the monthly media in order to focus more effort on particular **messages** or **journalists**. Practitioners will also evaluate the results of specific campaigns which will enable them to see if their original **objectives** have been met or not.

Evaluation helps **public relations** practitioners to identify likely dangers before they occur and helps to prove the worth of the overall campaign. In short, evaluation focuses effort, demonstrates effectiveness, ensures cost efficiency, encourages good management and facilitates accountability. It is important to evaluate outcome rather than output. For example, a heavy **press clippings** file may be desirable, but it is the effect of the **messages** contained

E

in the **press clippings** which is important. Effective evaluation should measure the change in people's **attitudes** after exposure to certain **public relations messages**. Evaluation may be **quantitative** or **qualitative** according to the methods used. It should also be continuous, i.e. garnered throughout the life of the campaign, be objective and be scientific. The terms listed below outline some of the evaluation processes used in a **public relations** programme:

- *Input*: refers to what a **public relations** practitioner does and how these products are distributed. For example, a **press release** may be written and sent. When evaluating inputs elements such as the quality of the background **research**, writing effectiveness and choice of distribution channels are measured.
- *Output*: refers to how the outputs are used by the target public. For example how many newspapers printed the key **message**. Measurement of output often concerns counting things.
- *Outcome*: refers to the measurement of the end effect of the communication. For example how many people changed their attitude of a result of reading the intended **message**. Outcomes are measured in three ways:
  1 changes at the thinking or awareness level (*cognitive*);
  2 changes in the attitude or opinion level (*affective*);
  3 changes in behaviours (*conative*).
- *Out-take*: refers to an intermediate position between an output and an outcome. It describes what a person may take and/or learn from a communications programme but it may not lead to further action which can be measured.

Watson, T. and Noble, P. (2005) *Evaluating Public Relations: A Best Practice Guide to Public Relations Planning, Research and Evaluation.* London: Kogan Page.

E

Events management

Events management is a typical **public relations tool** and found in many **public relations** campaigns. Special events are the phenomenon arising from non-routine occasions which have leisure, cultural, personal or organisational **objectives** set apart from the normal activity of daily life. Their purpose is normally to enlighten, celebrate, entertain or challenge the experience of a group of people. Events can be categorised into four types:

1 *leisure events*: leisure, sport, recreation;
2 *cultural events*: music, ceremonial, sacred and heritage events, art, folklore;

3 *organisational events*: commercial, political and charitable events, sales, **press receptions**;

4 *personal events*: weddings, birthdays, anniversaries.

Bowden *et al.* (2006) offer two definitions of special events:

1 a one-time or infrequently occurring event outside normal programmes or activities of the sponsoring organisation or body;

2 an opportunity for a leisure, social or cultural experience outside the normal range of choices or beyond everyday experiences.

Events are characterised according to their size and scale. Common categories are major events, mega-events, hallmark events and local/community events. Major events are events which will attract major media coverage and economic **benefits** such as the British Formula One Grand Prix and Cowes Week which is hosted on the Isle of Wight. Hallmark events refers to events which celebrate the ethos and spirit of the town or location. Classic examples are the Notting Hill Carnival in West London and the Tour de France. Mega-events, such as the Olympic Games or the FIFA World Cup, are so large that they affect whole economies and have international media coverage, while local or community events are targeted at the local population, notably for **fund-raising** or entertainment purposes. Events can also be categorised by form or content, as in the case of cultural, business and agricultural events.

There are a number of considerations a **public relations** practitioner needs to take into account when planning and managing an event, whether large or small. These can be communication-based, such as **media relations**, or logistical, such as decisions about location and **hospitality**.

See **sponsorship**.

Bowden, G. *et al.* (2006) *Events Management*, 2nd edn. Oxford: Butterworth-Heinemann.

Conway, D. (2006) *The Event Manager's Bible: How to Plan and Deliver an Event*. Oxford: How To Books.

E

Excellence theory

Public relations excellence is rooted in **stakeholder** theory and the **belief** that an organisation's success depends on the skill with which it manages the demands of its **stakeholders** and the success of its **relationship management**. Excellence is based in **two-way symmetrical communication.** By nature, an organisation is populated by various **publics** and **stakeholders** and an organisation must build good and mutually dependent relationships in order to survive. James **Grunig** (1992) postulated the excellence theory, suggesting that communication is fundamental to **public relations** excellence. **Two-way symmetrical communication** is based on dialogue and give-and-take between two parties. A relationship is built on interaction where both parties engage in the decision-making process and the sharing of ideas. Excellence suggests that communication helps the organisation to understand and to negotiate expectations, resulting in a **win–win** situation for both parties involved in the process. The key features of excellent **public relations** include strong cultures, **symmetrical communication** systems, empowering leadership, the decentralisation of **strategic planning**, entrepreneurship and social responsibility (Grunig, 1992)

The excellence approach in management has emerged with speed during the last few decades and can be explained as a response to environmental change, **globalisation** and the necessity for effectiveness of the **stakeholder** value.

Grunig, J. (ed.) (1992) *Excellence in Public Relations and Communication Management*. Mahwah, NJ: Lawrence Erlbaum.

Exhibitions

Exhibitions, displays, events and trade shows generally involve much time and planning but always carry a **public relations** benefit whether large or small, international or private view. From the **public relations** practitioners' point of view there are four aspects of involvement in exhibition work. They are:

1 **public relations** support at an exhibition stand;
2 setting up and running a stand at an exhibition;
3 organising an exhibition;
4 **public relations** exhibitions or displays.

Some key questions need to be answered before exhibiting at any event:

- What is the purpose of the exhibition?
- What **messages** about the organisation are to be conveyed?
- What **(corporate) image** does the organisation intend to display?
- How is this to be achieved?
- What is the **budget**?

If the role of the **public relations** department is to organise the exhibition itself, further **issue**s need to be taken into consideration, such as:

- booking the venue;
- arranging for all **publicity** and **promotion**;
- inviting potential exhibitors to participate;
- providing the contractor's manual;
- arranging the exhibition hall layout, provision of stand space, services, etc;
- manning a press office and providing information services.

See **events management, trade fairs.**

Expert prescriber

The **communication manager** is the second of two dominant roles within **public relations**, the first being the **communication technician**. The expert prescriber is one of three types of manager role within the **paradigm** of **communication manager**. The expert prescriber **research**es and defines **public relations** problems, develops programmes and implements them, often with the assistance of others in the team.

See **communication manager, communication technician.**

Extended picture caption

An extended picture caption is used when the picture itself is more important than the **press release** it accompanies. Here, when the picture is the real news item, a longer than usual explanatory caption is used to replace the **press release**.

External and internal review drivers

Regular **evaluation** and review of the **public relations programme/ plan** will often force adjustments to be made to the campaign. **Objectives** may be refocused and **tactics** may be altered. However, sometimes there is a need for major review if there are fundamental changes in the external or internal 'drivers'. The following list identifies some possible external drivers which may force a review:

- legislative changes which may either threaten or offer opportunities to the organisation;

E

- competitor changes which may either threaten or offer opportunities to the organisation;
- a takeover or acquisition;
- a major **product recall** or damage to corporate reputation;
- action by powerful pressure or activist groups.

Internal drivers may also force a review and these can include:

- corporate restructure with new priorities which affect the **public relations** function;
- changes in key personnel which affect the **public relations** function;
- **budget** changes which force changes to the **public relations** activities;
- future needs which may refocus the **public relations** function.

See **activism.**

External media support

There are often occasions when help is needed in the communication and distribution of information and **messages** from external agencies. There are two main agencies operating in the UK – the **Press Association** and **Reuters**. The **press release** and picture distribution services within these agencies enable the **public relations** practitioner to send **messages** and images straight into the newsrooms of the UK's media and to media overseas. There are two other methods of distribution using the internet. The **Press Association** uses PA Mediapoint (www.pamediapoiont-pr.press. net) and PA Picselect (www.papicselect.com). These services release **press release**s or download **image**s placed by customers. They are also able to host virtual pressrooms and have facilities to produce high-quality **promotion**al features to support any media campaign. **Reuters** has similar services available.

These press agencies distribute press directly into **editorial** newsrooms, using the same satellite links and lines as its **editorial**. This means that thousands of **news release**s can be seen at the same time on **editorial** screens throughout the UK.

See **Reuters.**

e-Zine

An e-zine is an electronic magazine which can be accessed either via a **website** or delivered directly to a user through their e-mail account.

See **on-line copywriting assignments.**

Face-to-face communication

Face-to-face communication is the best form of communication, especially in a conflict situation. Here, non-verbal communication cues can be assessed and can make a significant difference to the meaning of interactions. **Mutual understanding** is the primary aim of **public relations** and is important for the continued existence of good and beneficial relationships. Active listening **techniques** provide an easy way to establish if both parties understand the other's position. Collaboration only occurs in a climate of trust and this is encouraged by practising face-to-face interpersonal communication.

See **interpersonal communication.**

Hargie, O. (2006) *The Handbook of Communication Skills*, 3rd edn. London: Routledge.

Facility visits

Facility visits are used to help demonstrate a particular product or service to **journalist**s, often as part of **business to business (B2B) public relations**. Facility visits are also used in **crisis management** when **journalist**s are invited the view the aftermath and subsequent management of a particular **crisis**. Facility visits are most successful when precisely targeted to the trade press.

Fast-moving consumer goods (FMCGs)

FMCGs consist of a wide variety of high-demand consumer products sold at relatively low cost, e.g. light bulbs, cosmetics and cheap domestic appliances.

Feature articles

Unlike a **press release**, a feature article is an article written exclusively for one publication and cannot be reproduced anywhere else without permission. The article can be rewritten from a fresh perspective and with fresh examples to suit other journals, but each actual article will be an exclusive. A syndicated article is the name given to a feature article which is supplied to more than one publication. Also, unlike a **press release**, a feature article is unlikely to be seriously edited.

A feature article is an important **public relations tool** owing to its permanent value. Magazines are often retained in binders or in libraries, **articles** are often kept as part of the literature on the subject and reprints can be made for future use as **direct mail** or as material on show stands or for exhibition use. An article can have a long life because a magazine readership is substantially more than its circulation.

A feature article differs from a straight news story in one respect – its intent. While a news story provides information about an event, an idea or a situation, a feature does a bit more. It may also interpret news and add depth and colour to a story. It may instruct or entertain. The structure of a feature article is vitally important. The introduction should entice the readers, hook them in using drama, emotion, quotations, questions or descriptions. The body of the article must keep any promises and answer any questions raised in the introduction, while the conclusion should be written to help the reader remember the message of the story, sometimes with the aid of a strong punchline.

Points to keep in mind when writing a feature article:

- Focus on human interest – the feel and emotion demonstrated in the writing is crucial.
- Do not write the 'science' story – write the 'human interest' story.
- Be clear about the intention of the article. Is it to inform, persuade, observe, evaluate or evoke emotion?
- Write in the active voice. In active writing, people *do* things; in passive writing, things are done *to* people.
- Be accurate at all times – editors do check facts.
- Keep the **audience** in mind. What are their desires? What matters to them?
- Avoid clichés and sentimental statements.
- Use direct quotes to tell the story.
- Don't rely on the computer spellcheck.
- Decide on the tense and stick to it. The present tense works best in feature articles.

F

- Avoid lengthy, complex sentences and paragraphs. If the article appears in columns, one or two sentences equals a paragraph.
- Ideas come from everywhere – watch, read, listen, take notes, talk to people.

The lead or hook should invite the reader to read further and there are a number of types:

1 *Quick-burst lead*: opens with a series of short, direct statements.
2 *Surprise lead*: is an eye-opening beginning.
3 *Contrast lead*: opens with opposites or differences.
4 *Figurative lead*: opens with a figure of speech.
5 *Allusion lead*: opens with a reference to literature.
6 *Expert lead*: opens with a quote from an expert.
7 *Suspense lead*: has an open-ended suspense-filled beginning.
8 *Question lead*: begins with an opening question.

A well-**research**ed, readable article results from a wealth of information. Bad or boring **articles** result from too little information. Jefkins (1994) proposed a seven-point checklist for developing feature articles:

1 the opening paragraph;
2 the problem or previous situation;
3 the search for a solution or improvement;
4 the solution or improvement;
5 the results achieved;
6 the closing paragraph;
7 the draft checked with sources of information.

Ideas or themes for feature articles should always be suggested or **pitch**ed to an editor of a targeted publication and never written speculatively. Access to any information or interviewees should also be secured before approaching an editor with ideas. The proposition for a **public relations** feature article should present the idea, state that permission has been obtained to cover the subject and conduct the necessary **research** and suggest that if the editor likes the idea he/she should state the word count, the deadline for the copy and the date of the issue in which the article will appear.

F

Jefkins, F. (1994) *Public Relations Techniques*, 2nd edn. Butterworth-Heinemann.
Hennessy, Brendan (2006) *Writing Feature Articles*, 4th edn. Oxford: Focal Press.

Feedback

Feedback is a process of sharing ideas, **observation**s, concerns and suggestions between organisations and individuals. The intended outcome is to improve both personal and organisational performance.

See **asymmetrical communication, symmetrical communication.**

Financial public relations

Financial **public relations** is the management of communications between a listed company and its financial **audience**s (the City) and should not be confused with financial services **marketing** which is **public relations** for financial services companies such as banks or accountants. A listed company is a company whose shares are traded on the Stock Exchange. These companies are bound by rules and regulations affecting their activities and financial performance and are obliged to report back to their investors. The job of the financial **public relations** adviser is to help build an awareness and understanding of the company in the City and among **opinion formers and leaders** such as the media and analysts who influence both small and large investors and potential investors. The main purpose of financial **public relations** is to ensure that the share price of a company adequately reflects its value and to help liquidity in its shares. Potential investors are referred to as 'third-party' **audience**s and the relationship with them is unique to financial **public relations**.

City **audience**s are made up of people who have an interest or influence in the money markets. The main **audience**s which concern financial **public relations** are:

- institutional investors – existing shareholders, potential shareholders or past shareholders
- analysts
- private client stockbrokers
- private individuals
- the media
- the trade press
- wire services
- internet news services.

Holtz, S. (2002) *Public Relations on the Net: Winning Strategies to Inform and Influence the Media. The Investment Community, the Public and More,* 2nd edn. New York: Amacom.

Flow of influence concept

In 1948, Americans Lazarsfeld, Berelson and Gaudel theorised their concept of the 'flow of influence'. They suggested that there was a two-step flow of communication, claiming that ideas often flow from radio and print to **opinion formers and leaders** and from them on to the less active members of the general population. There are obvious implications of this in **public relations** terms because as **opinion formers and leaders** are generally dispersed among the population, it is hard to isolate and identify them. The best way to influence them is to inform the media which best reaches them. Rogers (1995) envisaged diffusion through a population as a communications process in which the content of the message which is exchanged is concerned with a new or novel idea. The essence of the diffusion process is the information exchange through which one individual communicates a new idea to one or several others. This part of the communication process – **interpersonal communication** or word of mouth – is normally outside the control of the organisation but not necessarily outside its influence. It is this influence that **public relations** practitioners seek to wield.

Lazarsfeld, P., Berelson, L. and Gaudet, T. (1948) *Propaganda and Communication in World History*, Vol. 2. Honolulu: University of Hawaii Press.

Rogers, M. R. (1995) *Diffusion of Innovations*, 4th edn. London: Macmillan.

Focus groups

A focus group is a form of **qualitative research** and is a discussion group consisting of carefully selected individuals. The idea behind a focus group is to encourage the participants to develop prompt responses and viewpoints to the relevant questions asked by the co-ordinator. Properly achieved, the focus group can elicit more information than **one-to-one interviews** and can result in great depth of insight and rewards. They are used by marketers and **public relations** practitioners to establish public perceptions and **attitudes** about an **issue**, organisation, service or product and are an effective use of **two-way symmetrical communication.** Questions are asked in an interactive group setting where participants are free to talk with other group members.

Variants of the focus group include:

- *the two-way focus group*: one focus group watches another focus group and discusses the observed interactions and conclusions;

F

- the *dual moderator focus group*: one moderator ensures that the session progresses smoothly, while another ensures that all topics are covered;
- the *duelling moderator focus group*: two moderators take opposite sides with regard to the **issue** under discussion;
- the *respondent moderator focus group*: one or more of the respondents are asked to act as the moderator temporarily;
- the *client participant focus group*: one or more client representatives participate in the discussion, either covertly or overtly;
- the *mini focus group*: groups are made up of four or five members rather than eight to twelve;
- the **teleconference** *focus group*: the telephone network is used;
- the *on-line focus group*: computers and the internet are used.

Although there are a number of advantages in using focus groups as a method of **qualitative research**, there are also several limitations and these include the following:

- The **research**er has less control over a group than a **one-to-one interview**.
- Data can be difficult to analyse.
- Time can be lost on **issue**s irrelevant to the topic.
- Moderators and observers need to be highly trained.
- A small sample is used.
- There is observer bias.

See **attitudes, beliefs, qualitative research methods, research, values.**

Barbour, R. (2007) *Doing Focus Groups*. London: Sage.
Litosseliti, L. (2003) *Using Focus Groups in Research*. London: Continuum.

F

Formal organisation

Formal organisation relates to the collection of work groups which have been consciously designed by senior management to maximise efficiency and achieve organisational goals.

See **informal organisation.**

Four Ps

The four Ps (Picture, Promise, Prove and Push) are a formula within the **motivating sequence**. A **copywriter** or **public relations** writer creates a picture of what the product or service can do for the reader, then promises that the picture will come true if the prospect buys the product, proves what the product has done for other customers and finally pushes for action.

See **AIDA model, BFD formula, motivating sequence.**

Freedom of the press

Freedom of the press is assumed to be a necessary part of any democratic society and is the guarantee by a government of free public press for its citizens and for members of news- gathering services and their published reporting. In developed countries, freedom of the press implies that all people should have the right to express themselves in writing or in other personal and creative ways. The Universal Declaration of Human Rights claims that 'Everyone has the right to freedom of opinion and expression; this right includes freedom to hold opinions … and impart information and ideas through any media regardless of frontiers.' According to Reporters Without Borders, more than a third of the world's people live in countries where there is no press freedom. More often than not, these people live in countries where there is no democratic system or where there are serious flaws in the democratic process.

Modern technological advances have huge implications for freedom of the press, especially in non-democratic countries. Satellite television is difficult to police and control, as is web-based publishing (**blog**ging). Voice over Internet Protocol systems can employ sophisticated encryption systems to evade central monitoring. As these technologies progress, they are likely to make the effective monitoring of **journalist**s and their contacts and activities a difficult task for governments.

There are restrictions on freedom of expression which should be considered by all **public relations** practitioners. They include the following:

- *Copyright*: this law forbids the use of other people's written words or illustrations without their consent. **Copyright** protection covers in general the author of the words, not the creator of the ideas. A person whose **copyright** is infringed can obtain a court order preventing further breach and can claim financial compensation.
- *Libel*: this is a false attack on someone's reputation. The courts can award very high damages for **defamation**. Any article

F

which contains personal criticism should be checked very carefully for truth of its content.

- *Slander*: this is an untrue spoken statement aimed at damaging someone's reputation and can also be the subject of legal action.
- *Contempt of court*: this covers threats to the administration of justice, including comments about trials in progress.
- *Obscenity*: this means material which tends to 'deprave or corrupt' and is a serious criminal offence.
- *Blasphemy*: this is the offensive treatment of the Christian faith and is a criminal offence, although it is rare for blasphemy charges to be brought today.
- *Privacy and **confidentiality***: there is no absolute right to privacy in English Law, but this does not prevent people, usually celebrities, attempting to take publications to court if they feel their privacy has been violated.
- *Racial hatred*: the use of threatening, abusive or insulting words intended or likely to stir up racial hatred is a crime. Very few prosecutions have been brought to date and the consent of the attorney-general is required but rarely granted.
- *Official Secrets*: this can mean the communication of almost any information acquired by civil servants under section 2 of the Official Secrets Act 1911.

Starr, P. (2004) *The Creation of the Media: Political Origins of Modern Communications*. New York: Basic Books.

Freelance consultant

A freelance **public relations** consultant is often employed by a **public relations consultancy** on an ad hoc basis to cover short-term assignments. They are also used to augment the in-house service from time to time. Their fees should be modest as overheads are low. Reputable freelance **public relations** consultants should belong to the **Chartered Institute of Public Relations (CIPR)**.

Freelance writers

Freelance writers are used on an ad hoc basis to support the writing-based work of a **public relations** department or consultancy. They are often employed to write **feature articles**, **scripts**, **press release**s and **speeches**.

Functionalism and public relations

Functionalism has been defined as 'Any view which analyses something in terms of how it functions, and especially in terms of its causes and effects' (Lacey, 1976, 83). Within the field of **public relations** a functionalist approach focuses on elements which assist organisations to function as integrated subsystems by maintaining consensus. In other words, a functionalist approach explores the **two-way symmetrical** role of communications and the resulting 'harmony' brought about by mutual adaptation.

Lacey, A. R. (1976) *A Dictionary of Philosophy*. London: Routledge.

Fund-raising

Fund-raising is a specialist **public relations** service designed to raise funds or other gifts in kind, particularly for a **not-for-profit** or charitable organisation. The primary aim of the **public relations** practitioner is to create an awareness of the organisation's service and to encourage individuals, grant-making trusts, businesses, charitable foundations and government agencies, both local and central, to donate funds to help the organisation carry out its mission, aims and **objectives**. Fund-raising activities can range from large grant appeals to small one-off events such as car washing or jumble sales.

Fitzherbert, L. (2003) *Effective Fundraising: An Informal Guide to Getting Donations and Grants*. London: Directory of Social Change.
Hart, Ted *et al.* (2005) *Non-Profit Internet Strategies: Best Practices for Marketing Communications and Fundraising Success*, Hoboken, NJ: Wiley.

F

Galley proofs

Proofs are the preliminary versions of publications. They may be in manuscript form or electronic. They are part of the early proof-reading and **copy-editing** process of communication material. Galley proofs are named thus because in the days when proofs were typeset by hand, the printer would set the page into metal frames known as 'galleys'. These would be used to print a small number of copies for mark-up and editing. The printer would then rearrange the type and print the final version. Some publishers send galley proofs out as reviews to magazines and libraries in advance of final publication. Proofs in electronic form are rarely sent out owing to the ease with which they may be edited and sent out under another author's name. Galley proofs sent nearer the final checking time are known as page proofs.

Game theory

Game theory provides a method for analysing strategic behaviour and explores how individuals and groups behave in a way which acknowledges the anticipated behaviour of others and the interdependence of the actors involved. The **Nash equilibrium model** suggests that by employing a **strategy** to reflect the **strategy** of the opposing side results in a **win–win** situation. In other words, both parties compromise in order to achieve what they want, rather than following their selfish interests. Nash equilibrium occurs when the organisation takes the best possible action given the action of the public and the public takes the best possible action given the action of the organisation, both parties, therefore, ending up with a satisfactory outcome. If the mutually beneficial relationship is to survive, co-operation and trust must exist.

See **win–win**.

Kreps, D. (1990) *Game Theory and Economic Modelling*. Oxford: Oxford University Press.

Gantt chart

A Gantt chart is a type of bar chart which illustrates a project breakdown or schedule and was first developed as a production tool by the social scientist Henry L. Gantt in 1817. Gantt charts show the start and finish dates of projects and the terminal and summary elements which constitute the breakdown of the project's structure. Gantt charts have become a common method of representing the work activities of a project to a wide **audience** and can also chart the dependency relationships between projects.

The steps in creating a Gantt chart are as follows:

1 *Tasks*: break down the work involved into individual tasks.
2 *Timelines*: set the **timeline** for each task. Both starting and completion times should be considered.
3 *Priority*: set the priority of the task and consider which other tasks need to be completed before starting a new one.
4 *Grid*: draw a grid with the days leading up to the event across the top and a list of the tasks down the left-hand side of the grid. A horizontal bar corresponding to each task is drawn across the grid.
5 *Milestones*: mark those tasks which are of particular importance in order to monitor the progress of the task.

Today, Gantt charts can be easily produced using software such as Microsoft Project or Excel. Figure 7 shows a simplified version of a Gantt chart relating to the distribution of a **press release**.

Tasks	M	T	W	T	F	S
Research	—					
Plan media			—			
Write					—	
Send						—

G

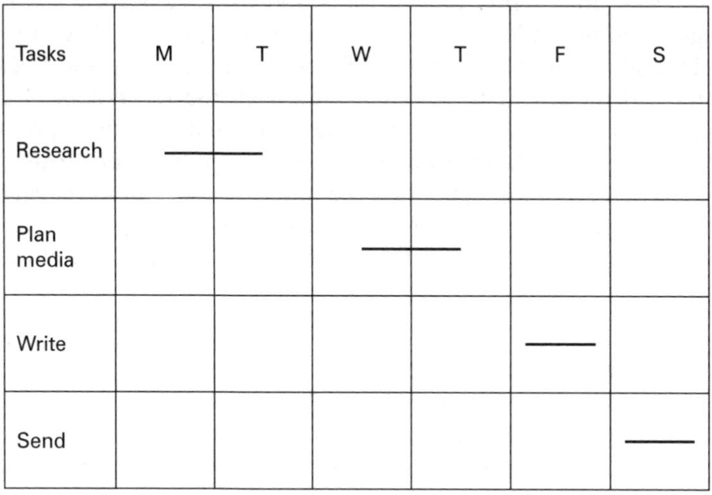

Figure 7   Gantt chart relating to the distribution of a press release

Gatekeeper

Journalists are often referred to as gatekeepers (of the news) because they have the power to decide which stories should be communicated to various **audience**s via the media. They therefore make value judgements about the importance of 'stories', which to place and where to place them. In effect, these gatekeepers of information have the power to structure what we think about.

> *See* **agenda-setting theory, opinion formers and leaders, Sapir-Whorf hypothesis.**

Globalisation

Simply put, globalisation can be described as a process by which the people of the world are unified into a single society through a combination of economic, technological, socio-cultural and political forces. The resulting 'global village' has enormous implications for global communicators. Today, the most compelling **issue** in global and **international public relations** is whether a global organisation can meet or exceed a myriad of voices and cultures without losing its identity by trying to be everything to all markets and to all publics. Although many similarities exist between what communicators would do domestically and what they would do globally, the differences can make or break the ability of an organisation to meet its strategic plans. These differences can include behaviour and **interpersonal communication** systems, culture and cultural differences, **mass media** structures and uses, **research** methodologies and an understanding of markets and public policy arenas. Globalisation has offered many new opportunities for **public relations** and the discipline has benefited from the technological and geopolitical changes which have delivered communicative opportunities with global **stakeholders**. In addition, **public relations** can be considered to have supported the process of globalisation via the spread of **values** and ideas through mass communication.

Globalisation affects **public relations** work in the following areas:

- It offers opportunities for the amalgamation of ideas, products and services for different countries.
- It increases opportunities for challenge and change.
- More organisations have international workforces and markets.
- **Public relations** is often associated with global power such as governments and international NGOs.

G

- Anti-globalisations require **public relations** services and diplomacy.

Dreher, A., Gaston, N. and Martens, P. (2008) *Measuring Globalisation: Gauging its Consequences*. New York: Springer.

Graphics

Graphics are visual interpretations intended to inform, illustrate or entertain, and can combine text, illustration and colour. They may be typography-based only, as in **brochures**, fliers, posters, **web-site**s and books. In **public relations**, clear and effective communication is the main objective of the use of graphics. Graphics can include drawing, painting, printmaking, line art, etching, illustrations, graphs, diagrams, symbols, geometrics, maps, photography, computer graphics and web graphics.

See **logo**.

JGA (2007) *1000 Retail Graphics from Signage to Logos and Everything In-store*. Gloucester, MA: Rockport.

Grassroots organisation

A grassroots organisation is one which is staffed by ordinary people, usually volunteers, for whom the aim of the organisation is close to their hearts. These organisations can be not-for-profit, philanthropical, political, religious or campaigning.

See **non-profit public relations**.

Greenwashing

'Greenwashing' and 'greening' are terms used to describe the act of misleading consumers regarding the environmental practices of a company or organisation. Greenwashing is a portmanteau of green and whitewash. The term is often used when more money has been spent on **advertising** the fact that the organisation is environmentally ethical than has actually been spent on green practices.

Stauber, J. and Rampton, S. (1995) *Toxic Sludge is Good for You! Lies, Damned Lies and the Public Relations Industry*. Monroe, ME: Common Courage Press.

G

Gregory (Anne)

Anne Gregory is Professor of Public Relations at Leeds Metropolitan University and the UK's only full-time professor in the subject area.

She is also Pro-Vice Chancellor and Director of the Centre for Public Relations Studies, a unique centre which brings together best practice on **research**, consultancy and teaching. She is an international speaker on a range of topics in **public relations** and holds visiting professor posts at a number of universities. Anne is an associate of DEMOS, the UK **think tank** and on the programme board for the UK Government's communication development initiative. Anne was President of the UK **Chartered Institute of Public Relations (CIPR)** in 2004. She has written extensively on **public relations** and authored numerous book chapters and papers in academic and practitioner publications. She edits the CIPR book series, 'PR in Practice', is editor-in-chief of the *Journal of Communication Management* and is on the board of *Ethical Space and Public Relations Review.*

Groupthink

'Groupthink' is the term used to describe the desire of a group of people not to disrupt the consensus. They try to minimise conflict without critically testing and evaluating ideas in order not to upset the comfort zone of consensual thought. A variety of reasons exist for groups engaging in groupthink, including a desire to avoid being seen as foolish or to avoid angering other members of the group. Groupthink may cause groups to make hasty or irrational decisions where the doubts of individuals are ignored for fear of upsetting the group's balance.

When groups become very cohesive, there is a danger that they will become victims of their own closeness. Irving Janis (1982) studied a number of American policy disasters and designed a chart of groupthink symptoms and prevention steps, as shown in Table 3.

Janis, I. L. (1982) *Victims of Groupthink: A Psychological Study of Foreign Policy Decisions and Fiascos*, 2nd edn. Boston, MA: Houghton Mifflin.

G

Table 3   Groupthink symptoms and prevention steps

Symptom	Prevention Steps
Illusion of invulnerability: members display excessive optimism that past successes will continue and will shield them and hence they tend to take extreme **risk**s.	The leader encourages open expression of doubt by members.

(Continued)

Table 3 Continued

Symptom	Prevention Steps
Collective rationalisation: members collectively rationalise away data which disconfirm the assumptions and **beliefs** upon which they base their decisions.	The leader accepts criticism of his/her opinions.
Illusion of morality: members believe that they as moral individuals are unlikely to make bad decisions.	Higher-status members offer opinions last.
Shared stereotypes: members dismiss disconfirming evidence by discrediting its source (e.g. stereotyping other groups and its leaders as evil or weak).	Recommendations are sought from a duplicate group.
Direct pressure: imposition of verbal, non-verbal or other sanctions on individuals who explore deviant positions (e.g. those who express doubts or question the validity of group **beliefs**) and perhaps the use of assertive language to force compliance.	The group is periodically divided into subgroups.
Self-censorship: members keep silent about misgivings with regard to the apparent group consensus and try to minimise their doubts.	Members seek the reactions of trusted outsiders.
Illusion of unanimity: members conclude that the group has reached a consensus because its most vocal members are in agreement.	Trusted outsiders are invited to join the discussion periodically.
Mindguards: members who take it upon themselves to screen out adverse, disconfirming information supplied by 'outsiders' which might endanger the group's complacency.	Someone is assigned the role of devil's advocate. Scenarios of rivals' possible actions are developed.

Source: Based on Janis (1982).

G

Grunig (James)

James E. Grunig, Ph.D., Professor Emeritus, is a celebrated **public relations** theorist. He is the co-author of *Managing Public Relations*, *Public Relations Techniques, Manager's Guide to Excellence in Public Relations and Communication Management* and *Excellent Public Relations and Effective Organisations: A Study of Communication Management in Three Countries*. He was editor of *Excellence in Public Relations and Communication Management*.

Grunig was named the first winner of the Pathfinder Award for Excellence in academic **research** in **public relations** by the of Institute Public Relations Research and Education in 1984. In 1989 he received the Outstanding Educator Award for the Public Relations Society of America. He won the most prestigious lifetime award of the Association for Education in Journalism and Mass Communication in 2000, the Paul J. Deutschmann Award for Excellence in Research. In 2002 he was awarded the James W. Schwartz Award for Distinguished Service to Journalism and Communication, Iowa State University. In 2005 he received the highest award of the Institute for Public Relations – the Alexander Hamilton Medal for Lifetime Contributions to Professional Public Relations.

Grunig's **research** has added many new theories to the existing body of **public relations** knowledge, most notably his **four models of public relations**, his **situational theory of publics** and his discussions of **two-way symmetrical communication**.

See **Grunig's four models of public relations, situational theory of publics, symmetrical communication.**

Grunig, J. E. and Hunt, T. (1984) *Managing Public Relations*. Orlando, FL: Harcourt Brace.

G

Grunig's four models of public relations

James **Grunig** and Todd Hunt (1984) developed their seminal models of **public relations** to help explain the history of formal **public relations** and how it is practised today. Table 4 summarises four **public relations** models: **press agentry/publicity, public information, two-way asymmetrical communication and two-way symmetrical communication**.

The **press agentry/publicity** model serves a **propaganda** function. Practitioners communicate information about the organisation or client through incomplete information, half truths or sometimes complete lies.

Table 4 Summary of Grunig's four models of public relations

Characteristic	Press agentry/ publicity	Public information	Two-way asymmetrical communication	Two-way symmetrical communication
	Propaganda	Dissemination of information	Scientific **persuasion**	**Mutual understanding**
Purpose				
Nature of communication	One-way: complete truth not essential	One-way: truth important	Two-way: imbalanced effects	Two-way: balanced effects
Communication model	Source to receiver	Source to receiver	Source to receiver to source	Source group to receiver group to source group
Nature of **research**	Little: 'counting house'	Little: readability, readership	Formative: evaluative of **attitudes**	Formative: evaluative of understanding
Leading historical figures	P. T. Barnum	Ivy **Lee**	Edward L. **Bernays**	Educators, professional leaders
Where practised today	Sports, theatre, product **promotion**	Government, non-profit associations, business	Competitive business	Regulated business
Estimated percentage of organisations practising today	15%	50%	20%	15%

Source: Adapted from Grunig and Hunt (1984).

G

The **public information model** serves to disseminate information about the organisation to the public objectively, rather like a '**journalist** in residence'. The intent is not necessarily persuasive.

The intent of **two-way asymmetrical communication** is scientific **persuasion**. Practitioners rely on what they know from social science theory and **research** on **attitudes** and behaviour to persuade **publics** to accept the organisation's point of view and to change their behaviour to support the organisation's point of view.

The final model – **two-way symmetrical communication** – is often referred to as 'excellent public relations', (see **excellence theory**). Here, practitioners act as mediators between organisations and their **publics.** The goal is **mutual understanding** between an organisation and its **publics**. Practitioner of this model use theories of communication rather than theories of **persuasion** when planning and evaluating **public relations** campaigns and communications.

Development of the four models in history:

- **press agentry/publicity**:   1850–1900
- **public information**:   1900–1920
- **two-way asymmetrical communication**:   1920s–
- **two-way symmetrical communication**:   1960s/70s–

Organisations which generally practise the **press agentry/ publicity** model equate **public relations** with **publicity** and **promotion**s. Practitioners concentrate on securing media attention for their clients. The best examples today include celebrities and music **promotion**, sports **promotion**, theatre and film, and product **promotion** in **advertising** departments. About 15 per cent of today's practitioners practise this model.

The **public information model** is the model most often practised today. **Grunig** and Hunt suggest that about 50 per cent of today's practitioners follow this model. It is popular in government agencies, educational establishments, not-for-profit agencies and many businesses.

The **two-way asymmetrical** model is mostly practised in business, especially companies concerned with consumer goods and those facing heavy competition. It is also practised by many **public relations consultancies**, especially those providing complementary services to **advertising**. **Grunig** and Hunt suggest that it is practised by about 20 per cent of practitioners.

Two-way symmetrical communication is mostly practised by professional **public relations** organisations and advised by **public**

relations educators. **Grunig** and Hunt suggest that it is practised in reality by 15 per cent of practitioners.

It is important to remember that these models are not mutually exclusive and are fluidly practised by many organisations and **public relations** practitioners. The models present a simplistic formula to aid general understanding of the ways in which **public relations** can be managed.

See **excellence theory**.

Grunig, J. E. and Hunt, T. (1984) *Managing Public Relations*. Orlando, FL: Harcourt Brace.

G

Halo effect

The 'halo effect' refers to the notion that an organisation's beneficial activities and the perceptions of these activities produce goodwill and that this goodwill can theoretically be transferred to other areas of the organisation's activities or products. If consumers are impressed by the environmental standing of the organisation, for example, they may well be persuaded to buy some of its products or use its services further. Thus the halo effect will transfer a positive **image** and improve customer's confidence in the organisation.

The opposite of the halo effect is the 'horns effect', which takes the view that everything bad about an organisation is based on a single instance.

Headlines

Headlines do more than attract attention. They perform four different tasks:

1 They attract attention.
2 They select the **audience**.
3 They deliver a complete **message**.
4 They draw the reader into the body copy.

Headlines appeal to the reader's interests or desires but must also be valid and credible. Headlines are particularly important for **public relations** practitioners to consider when designing for **press releases**.

There are eight basic headline types:

1 Direct headlines which state the **unique selling proposition** directly with no hidden meanings or unnecessary word play.
2 Indirect headlines which make the point in a roundabout way in order to raise curiosity, which is later satisfied in the body copy.
3 News headlines which state important news about the product or service.

4 How-to headlines which offer the promise of solid information or solutions to problems.

5 Question headlines with which the reader can empathise.

6 Command headlines which generate sales by telling readers what to do.

7 Reason-why headlines which list the features of the product or service in a 1, 2, 3 style.

8 **Testimonial** headlines where previous customers do the selling by supporting and endorsing the product or service.

See **copywriting.**

Heath (Robert)

Professor Robert L. Heath has published twelve books and almost a hundred **articles** and chapters on **communication theory, rhetoric, public relations, issues management** and **crisis** communication. He is currently Professor of Communication specialising in public relations at the University of Houston. He lectures on the above topics throughout the world.

Heath, R. L. (ed.) (2001) *Handbook of Public Relations*. Thousand Oaks, CA: Sage.

Hegemony

Hegemony is a concept which describes the dominance of one social group over another such that the ruling group acquires some degree of consent from the subordinate without the use of force or power. In a **public relations** context the ideal of the hegemonic group may be inculcated in the populace through education, **advertising, influence** and **persuasion** and publications. Theories of hegemony attempt to explain how dominant or individuals maintain their power and the capacity of dominant classes to persuade subordinate ones to accept, adopt and internalise their **views** and norms.

Hierarchy

Hierarchy relates to the number of levels of authority found in an organisation.

See **organisational chart, organisational structure, organisational structure of public relations, span of control.**

Hierarchy of needs

The hierarchy of needs was a model put forward by American psychologist Abraham Maslow (see Figure 8). The basis of the model is that individuals have fundamental needs or desires which they will seek to satisfy. In addition they will have an in-built system aimed to prioritise these needs and wants.

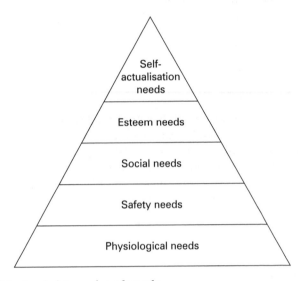

Figure 8   Maslow's hierarchy of needs

The five levels in the hierarchy of needs can be defined in the following way:

1 *Physiological needs:* these include the wide range of needs of individuals in order to be able to function on a daily basis. They include the need for food, air to breathe, water to drink, and sleep. In an organisational setting this would include the need for wages.
2 *Safety needs:* these include needs which provide security for the individual, such as the need to be free from harm and the need for shelter. In an organisational setting this would include the need for job security.
3 *Social needs:* these include needs which draw on the social support necessary for life, such as friendship, family and a sense of belonging. In an organisational setting this would include the need to work as part of a team.

4 *Esteem needs*: these include the need for self-respect and feelings of achievement, recognition and reputation. In an organisational setting this would include the need for formal recognition by management for useful contributions.

5 *Self-actualisation needs:* this includes the need for individuals to reach their full potential and to have significant influence over their life. In an organisational setting this would include having the freedom to organise one's working life to suit personal circumstances and to be managed on the basis of ends rather than means.

Maslow suggests that the elements in the model should not be considered as totally fixed. He suggests that the hierarchy of needs displays the following properties:

1 A need once satisfied is no longer a motivator.
2 A need cannot be effective as a motivator until those before it in the hierarchy have been satisfied.
3 If deprived of the source of satisfaction from a lower order need, it will once more become a motivator.
4 There is an in-built desire to work up the hierarchy.
5 Self-actualisation is unlike the other needs – there are no boundaries within the need itself.

Maslow, A. (1943) 'A theory of human motivation', *Psychological Review*, 50, 370–396.
Martin, J. (2005) *Organizational Behaviour and Management*, 3rd edn. London: Thomson, 433–436.

Hollis public relations

Hollis Public Relations is an internet search engine for the **public relations** industry. It allows an individual to find a **public relations consultancy**, source an **in-house public relations** contact, locate a specialist service, search for a media contact and look for a job in **public relations**.

www.hollis-pr.com

Hospitality

Hospitality refers to the practice of 'looking after' various **stakeholders,** for example providing catering facilities and accommodation during events, **facility visits** and **conferences**, etc. There are strong links between hospitality and **networking, relationship-building** and **reputation management**.

See **events management.**

Hot-issue publics

Hot-issue publics are a subset of an organisation's overall **publics** and are a further division of an organisation's **active publics**. They are those **publics** involved in an **issue** which has a great deal of public support and much media attention and amplification surrounding it. It is important for **public relations** practitioners to consider this group of publics very carefully in their **issues management** planning.

See **active publics, issues management, publics.**

House journals

A house journal is the particular journal or magazine published by an organisation. It includes news, events and views about the organisation itself, often with contributions written by members and employees of the organisation and is a **tool** of internal **public relations**.

Hypodermic needle model

The hypodermic needle model of media effect, also known as the magic bullet perspective, emerged from the Marxist Frankfurt School of intellectuals in the 1960s to explain the rise of Nazism in Germany. The communications model claims that an intended **message** is wholly and passively accepted by the receiver and that **mass media** has a direct and immediately powerful effect on its **audience**s. The hypodermic needle illusion is intended to give a mental **image** of a direct and strategic infusion of a **message** into an individual. However, the one fatal flaw of the hypodermic needle model is that it ignores matters of interpretation of meaning, which is an essential aspect of the communicative process.

See **Osgood Schramm model of communication, Shannon and Weaver.**

H

Ideology

An ideology is an organised collection of ideas or abstract thought or a way of 'looking at things'. The term was coined in the late eighteenth century to define a 'science of ideas'. An ideology is often a set of ideas which is proposed by the dominant class of a society and then adopted by all members of that society. The purpose of ideology is to change society through normative thought processes. An understanding of ideological practices is important to **public relations** professionals when considering how a new public's dominant ideological meaning systems affect its public communication efforts with relevant and conflicting **publics**.

Hawks, D. (2003) *Ideology*, 2nd edn. London: Routledge.

Image

An organisation's image relates to its public 'face'. Images can be manufactured, changed and managed. In the broadest sense, image is the impression people have as a result of their knowledge and experience of the organisation. Five different types of images are listed below:

1 *Mirror image*: relates to the way in which internal managers think outsiders see the organisation.
2 *Current image*: established through **situation analysis**. This is the image actually held by outsiders and may well differ from the mirror image.
3 *Wish image*: relates to an organisation which repositions itself and wishes to create a new image. The danger is that an organisation may project an overenthusiastic or biased image.
4 *Multiple image*: occurs when representatives of the organisation each create a personal image of the organisation so that there are as many images as there are people. The answer to this dilemma is sales training to establish uniform behaviour.

5 *Optimum image*: occurs when a subject is very complicated. This kind of image hopes to give an accurate impression of something very technical or complicated – a layman's view.

6 *Corporate image*: see **corporate image**.

Image study

Image study is a form of **research** which looks for comparisons between the sponsor and rival organisations. This is often done via prearranged **interviews** with the buyers or decision-makers of an industrial product who are asked their opinions of the different organisations on a range of **issue**s. The results can then be presented in tables which list the name and number of respondents, the average score given to an **issue** and the standard deviation.

Implementation fees

Implementation fees cover the amount of time it takes a **public relations** practitioner or executive to implement the agreed campaign or **public relations programme/plan**. For ongoing programmes this is often based on a fixed amount of time per month.

Impression management

Impression management argues that people strategically use communication to create desired impressions of themselves or their organisations. In **public relations**, impression management is typically referred to as **image** or **reputation management**. Many organisations use impression management to repair an **image** tarnished by a **crisis**. A **crisis** is a mistake or miscue which can reflect badly on an organisation and become a threat to its **reputation**. When people or organisations make mistakes, they offer accounts, **messages** and communications about themselves designed to explain the event and influence positive perceptions of themselves.

See **reputation management**.

Rosenfeld, P., Giacalone, R. A. and Riordan, Catherine A. (1995) *Impression Management in Organisations, Theory, Measurement, Practice*. London: Routledge.

Industrial relations

Public relations has a major role to play in industrial relations: it ensures that management's perspective is heard and monitors how the organisation is perceived in the media during periods of industrial action.

Influence (laws of)

Kevin Hogan (2005) says that gaining the co-operation and compliance of other people is absolutely critical to the **persuasion** process and the continuance of society as we know it. He suggests ten laws of **influence** which would help the **public relations** practitioner to persuade a prospect. They are as follows:

1 *Law of Reciprocity*: give away something of perceived value to someone and others will feel compelled to do the same. This is where the free sample can come in handy.
2 *Law of Time:* in order to prevent prospects from concentrating on mistakes from the past, the **public relations** practitioner should get them to see things from a future perspective.
3 *Law of Contrast*: prospects should be shown the product believed to be the best option and/or least expensive last. They are compelled to own something and will normally take the least expensive item if it is shown last.
4 *Law of Friends*: the **public relations** practitioner should help prospects see him/her as a friend who cares about them. This will increase the probability of their compliance.
5 *Law of Expectancy*: the behaviours expected of oneself and others are more likely to be manifested in reality. If the **public relations** practitioner believes that prospects will most certainly buy into the idea of the product or service, they probably will.
6 *Law of Consistency*: prospects' past decisions and public proclamations dramatically influence their **beliefs, attitudes** and behaviours.
7 *Law of Association*: prospects should be allowed to see the product or service linked to the respected, the famous and the experienced.
8 *Law of Scarcity*: prospects believe that the value of something that they desire is greater if it is in short supply than if it were freely available.
9 *Law of Conformity*: prospects should be encouraged to see their future after purchasing the product or service as one where their peers and family approve of and are excited by their purchase.

10 *Law of Power*: people have power over other people if they are perceived to have greater authority, strength and expertise. Prospects are more likely to be influenced by others who act with confidence.

Hogan, K. (2005) *The Science of Influence*. Hoboken, NJ: Wiley.

Infoganda

Infoganda is a form of **propaganda** in which the message is delivered in a format which imitates an **infomercial**. The combination of an **infomercial** and **propaganda** is an advertisement or communication which pretends to be neutral (typically presenting itself as a news source) but which has an agenda of promoting a biased viewpoint of a large organisation. Infoganda is typical of a religious or governmental organisation.

See **infomercial, infotisement, propaganda.**

Infomercials

Infomercials present themselves as advertisements which run for as long as television programmes. They are also known as 'paid programming' or 'teleshopping'. They normally present a large amount of information in an effort to persuade viewers to a certain point of view. The content is a commercial message designed to represent the interests of the sponsor. They are designed to elicit a direct response and therefore are a form of direct response **marketing**.

See **infoganda, propaganda.**

www.responsemagazine.com

Informal organisation

An informal organisation is the network of relationships which spontaneously establish themselves between members of the organisation on the basis of their common goals or friendships.

See **formal organisation.**

Infotisement

An infotisement is a print article which looks like an objective piece of journalism but is in fact an advertisement, the ultimate aim of which is to sell the products or services referred to in the article. As a result, the validity of the content of the infotisement may be questioned.

See **infomercial, propaganda.**

In-house public relations

The majority of **public relations** practitioners work in-house – that is they work within the organisation itself, promoting its products and services rather than working in a **public relations consultancy** on various clients' campaigns. The reason for the dominance of the in-house practitioner practising **internal communications** is the attraction of the intimate knowledge they must have of the organisation and the understanding of its communication systems. In-house **public relations**, also known as internal **public relations**, has both its advantages and limitations.

Advantages:

- It offers a full-time service.
- It has good lines of communication.
- It has continuity of personnel.
- It offers better value for money.
- It offers proximity and access.

Limitations:

- There is a lack of impartiality.
- There is a narrower range of experience and possible lack of training.
- There is sometimes a poor person specification and/or job description owing to a lack of understanding of the true nature of **public relations**.
- There is a lack of varied experience.

See **Public Relations Consultants Association (PRCA).**

Inoculation theory

See **resistance.**

Integrated marketing communications (IMC)

IMC represents a holistic view of **marketing communications**. It is a planning process designed to assure that all **brand** contacts received by a customer or prospect for a product, service or organisation are relevant to that person and consistent over time. IMC is a management concept designed to make all aspects of **marketing** communication including **advertising, public relations, sales promotion** and direct **marketing** work together as a unified force with the same end goal, rather than as separate disciplines. There are several reasons for the recent rise in the popularity of IMC.

- the shift from media a**dvertising** to multiple forms of communication such as **promotion**s, **product placements**, **direct mail**, etc;
- the shift from **mass media** to more specialised media centred around specific and targeted **audience**s;
- the shift from a manufacturing-dominated market to a service- and retail-dominated market;
- the shift from general **marketing** and advertising to data-based **marketing**;
- the shift from traditional payment and compensation to performance-based pay and compensation;
- the shift from limited internet access to widespread internet availability.

IMC implies that there is non-duplication of effort. However, it is important that **messages** from **advertising, promotion**s and **public relations** dovetail and that a standard **image** be presented throughout.

Skinner *et al.* (2004, 51) suggest that a successful integrated **marketing** communication model requires:

- building a database of information on both customers and prospects (consider their **demographics, psychographics** and purchase history, and whether they are loyal consumers of the **brand** in question);
- formulating a contact management policy to determine what will be communicated about the product or service and the conditions under which the communication will be delivered;
- developing a communications **strategy** and deciding how the **message** will be delivered, given the context in which it will appear;
- setting **marketing objectives** which will vary between **brand**-loyal customers and competitive users;
- selecting the various **techniques** to achieve the established **marketing** and communication **objectives**, including **direct marketing, advertising, sales promotion, public relations** and **sponsorship**.

Skinner, A., von Essen, L. and Mersham, G. (2004) *Handbook of Public Relations*, 7th edn. Oxford: Oxford University Press.

Interactive media

Interactive media include the growing array of communication options which allow people to communicate with organisations using electronic equipment and telecommunications. Modern **audience**s now use interactive media technology in a variety of ways to make enquiries, perform many routine tasks and exchange information with organisations electronically. PCs are now not the only way to access the internet, e-mail or communication systems. Links through wireless applications protocol mobile phones are possible using the phone's screen and keypad. Storing and processing data, accessing **databases**, surfing the web, storing telephone directories and text-messaging are all possible. Wireless fidelity enables laptops and personal data assistants to connect wirelessly to the internet. Interactive television now converges with the internet. Technology is progressing at a rapid speed with new technological devices being invented constantly. To work effectively, **public relations** practitioners must keep up with the pace of technological change and understand the needs of the new media for information. The public's increased access to information has consequences for organisations – their **audience**s will not longer be passive; their activity can make or break an organisation's **reputation**.

See **blog, video blog (vlog), website, XPRL.**

Internal communications

One of the most important groups of **stakeholders** is an organisation's employees. Organisational **rhetoric** often claims that the organisation's employees are 'their greatest asset'. Keeping employees informed and empowered is a vital part of internal communications. A study by the *Journal of Marketing* stated that 68 per cent of customers defect from an organisation because of staff **attitudes** and indifference (Cowlett, 1999). Conversely, another survey carried out by MORI/MCA in 1999 found that 41 per cent of customers said they were more likely to buy a company's products or services again if staff treated them well, regardless of **advertising**, **brand**ing or **promotion**al activity. Employees are not a homogeneous group of **stakeholders**; they are the workers, management and board, all of whom perform different functions but need to be communicated with. Communication operates in many ways within an organisation. It can flow downwards from senior directors and management to workers, or upwards from the shop floor and between groups and individuals.

The goals of internal communications are to identify and maintain mutually beneficial relationships between the organisation and its employees on whom its success or failure depends. Communication with employees is vital:

- when attracting or inducting new employees;
- when instruction, news and job-related information should be disseminated;
- when rewards and recognition should be given, perhaps in the form of **promotion**s or awards;
- when employees' **contracts** are to be terminated.

Internal communications have advanced substantially from the internal **newsletter** of yesteryear. There are a number of reasons for this.

- There is now a greater requirement for organisations to inform their employees about policy decisions and financial affairs, including the **Annual Report**.
- There is an increasing democratisation of industry, especially in Europe. Employee ownership of company equity is increasing through privatisations, flotation, management buy-outs, performance-related pay schemes, etc.
- New communications technology, such as **intranet website**s, video magazines, **webcasts**, business TV, journals, teleconferencing, mobile telephones, e-mail, SMS and text-messaging, make it easier to organise and conduct internal audits.
- Many Western economies are now realising the importance and value of service and knowledge-based industries.

Internal **public relations techniques** fall under three headings: upwards communication (employee–management), sideways communication (employee–employee), and downwards communication (management–employee).

Upwards communication **techniques** can include readers' letters, suggestion schemes, house journal **articles** and specialist workshops. Sideways communication **techniques** can include classified house journal advertisements, staff clubs and social events, and staff news. Downwards communication **techniques** can include **Annual Report**s, company policy documents, appointment announcements, **corporate identity** and corporate **advertising**, the house journal, and cascade briefing sessions.

Cowlett, M. (1999) 'Creating a breed of company converts', *PR Week*, 9 Apr., 13–14.

Theaker, A. (2001) *The Public Relations Handbook*. Abingdon: Routledge, Ch. 11 – Internal Communications.

International news broadcasters

Below is a selection of the major players in international broadcasting to which all **public relations** practitioners in global affairs should have access:

- CNN International – a US-based news channel, known as the pioneer of 24-hour international news broadcasting and owned by Time Warner.
- **BBC** World – one of the **BBC** channels which offers in-depth news, sport, business and current affairs.
- Sky News - an independent television channel which offers in-depth news, sport, business and current affairs.
- Channel News Asia – an international news broadcaster based in Singapore.
- Al-Jazeera English – based in Dohar, Qatar.
- CCTV9 – based in China.

International public relations/communication

As new communication technologies and the **globalisation** of business has occurred, more and more **public relations** practitioners have recognised the need to be able to communicate effectively with international **audience**s. International **public relations** describes **public relations** which has an international focus and is often carried out in **consultancies** which are based in other countries or which have bought out local **consultancies** in order to capitalise from the cultural knowledge of local practitioners. International **public relations** presents many exciting opportunities, but it also faces challenges such as the differences in societal cultures. International **public relations** must reflect the cultural and societal norms of the host nation. Language can present problems and the corporate **slogans**, **marketing** and **advertising** themes need to be adjusted to suit the sensibilities of an international **audience**. Media may present challenges for international **public relations** because in many parts of the world governments continue to dominate media ownership. There are also **issue**s of **ethics** in the international arena to consider. International **public relations** forces practitioners to look beyond their own assumptions, environments and legal and ethical standards.

Curtin, P. A. and Gaither, T. K. (2007) *International Public Relations, Negotiating Culture, Identity and Power*. Thousand Oaks, CA: Sage.

Moss, D. and DeSanto, B. (eds) (2002) *Public Relations Cases, International Perspectives*. London: Routledge.

Internet groups

Internet groups are the visitors to an organisation's **website** who are used to gather information for **research** purposes. They can be asked to complete short **questionnaires** or to make comments on various organisational **issue**s via bulletin boards or chat rooms.

Interpersonal communication

Simply put, interpersonal communication is the process of sending and receiving information between two or more people. It comprises such variables as speech communication, non-verbal communication, unconscious communication, summarising, paraphrasing, listening, questioning, initiating and turn-taking. The term is used to define a concept which describes a method of influencing one another's behaviours beyond what can be attributed to normal baselines of action. Interpersonal communication is defined by mutual influence and as such is an important method of producing change from **public relations programmes/plans**. It is a method of communicating one-on-one in a dialogic fashion, one-on-group or group-on-group.

There are, however, a number of factors which can act as barriers to effective interpersonal communication:

- *Emotions*: extreme emotions are most likely to hinder interpersonal communications because the idea or message may be misinterpreted.
- *Filtering*: the sender can manipulate the information sent to the receiver in order to present a favourable message.
- *Information overload*: too much information on the same subject can be confusing.
- *Defensiveness*: individuals reject **mutual understanding** when they are defensive or feel under attack.
- *Cultural difference*: differing cultures and cultural awareness can hinder communications.
- *Jargon*: the use of jargon can be inhibiting.

The most effective interpersonal communicators simplify their language, constrain their emotions, listen actively and offer **feedback**.

See **questionnaires.**

Hargie, O. (2006) *The Handbook of Communication Skills*. London: Routledge.

Intervening publics

Intervening publics are specific groups who carry a message to the **primary publics** and **opinion leaders and formers**.

See **publics.**

Interviews (media)

Public relations practitioners engage in different types of interview. They may be interviewed themselves as representatives of their organisation or client or they may interview other people. Interviews may be for publications such as newspapers, magazines or **house journals**, they may be electronic as for **websites** or the internet, or they may be broadcast on radio or television. All interviews need to be prepared for – great interviews are both an art and a science. **Research** is paramount. If the **public relations** practitioner is interviewing he/she should:

- prepare and **research** questions;
- determine the goals of the interview;
- listen and respond to the interviewee;
- start light;
- climb the **news pyramid**;
- ask **open questions**;
- ask the interviewee for clarification;
- observe time limits;
- record the interview;
- make eye contact;
- thank the interviewee.

See **interviews (on-line).**

Bland, M., Theaker, A. and Wragg, D. (2005) *Effective Media Relations*, 3rd edn. London: Kogan Page.

Corfield, Rebecca (2006) *Successful Interview Skills: How To Present Yourself with Confidence*, 4th edn. London: Kogan Page.

Interviews (on-line)

On-line interviews are used as a **research** methodology and are an effective method of harvesting information from **stakeholders**.

They are quick, inexpensive and convenient. Other advantages include the fact that there is no **gatekeeper** – on-line interviews enable the **research**er to communicate directly with decision-makers, there is less interviewer bias because the interviewee cannot be interrupted and therefore has more time for thoughtful considerations, there is no time constraint and the interviewee can come back to complete the interview at any time.

Persichitte *et al.* (1997) recommend the following methodological guidelines when conducting e-mail interviews:

- Select the sample carefully.
- Establish guidelines with the interviewees.
- Establish a rapport with the interviewees prior to actual interviewing.
- Be timely with responses.
- Use acronyms and symbols which communicate feelings and emotions.
- Summarise the interviewee's responses to previous questions and return the summary to the interviewee immediately for verification.
- Check for **messages** from interviewees regularly.
- Break questions into small chunks.
- Be alert for misunderstandings.
- Study the culture of electronic mail – and don't be rude.

See **interviews (media).**

Persichitte, K. A., Young, S. and Tharp, D. D. (Feb. 1997) 'Conducting research on the internet, strategies for electronic interviewing'. Paper presented at the meeting of the Association for Educational Communications and Technology, Albuquerque, NM.

Intranet

An intranet is an organisation's internal **website** and is used as a tool of **internal communications**. It is used to promote common corporate and **organisational culture** and enhance collaboration resulting in workforce productivity. Intranets differ from extranets in that they are generally restricted to employees at the organisation, whereas extranets can generally be accessed by customers, suppliers and other approved parties.

Investor relations

See **financial public relations.**

Ipsos MORI

Ipsos MORI is the second-largest survey **research** organisation in the UK, formed by two of the leading companies in October 2005. The organisation has a freely available archive of **opinion polls** and public **attitude research** from 1970 onwards, including **trends**, on its **website**. The company also specialises in media, loyalty and **marketing** and **advertising research**.

See **Mintel, secondary research.**

www.ipsos-mori.com

Issue

An issue can be defined as a topic for debate, a **trend** or a recurring theme or situation which moves from the private sphere into the **public sphere** and subsequently on to the media agenda.

See **crisis, crisis management, issues management.**

Issues management

Issues management is a principal focus on **techniques** for anticipating, planning and proactively managing **issue**s to minimise negative commercial impact and create competitive opportunities. According to Chase and Jones (1979), issues management is also a **tool** which companies could use to identify, analyse and manage emerging **issue**s (in a populist society experiencing discontinuous change) and respond to them *before* they become public knowledge. They considered that

> when challenged by today's **activism**, business tends to react to overt symptoms, rather than identifying and analysing fundamental causes of the **trend** which has led to a critical i**ssue**. It is not surprising then, that when a critical **issue** reaches the public policy decision-making point, business finds itself the defendant in the court of **public opinion**.

While issues management may be considered by some to be an integral part of **strategic planning** and a basic ingredient for corporate survival, it is considered by others to imply the manipulation of events or conditions which freely occur in pluralistic and democratic societies.

Issues management suggests that there are dynamic forces, political, regulatory, economic, social and technological, which shape the way in which organisations work and that any changes in these forces expand:

- the quality, quantity and speed of information globally;
- the impact of new broadcast and multimedia technologies on **public opinion**;
- the competition for influencing customers;
- the knowledge, value and behaviour of constituents;
- the association between product and **brand** reputation.

The main **issue**s which concern **public relations** practitioners are:

- safety and security;
- the environment (including the workplace);
- gender and equality;
- service quality and value for money;
- institutional accountability;
- empowerment.

Changes in any of these areas can result in an increase in **activism**, including picketing, boycotting and litigating – at which stage the **issue** becomes a **crisis**. The key questions facing practitioners in relation to an emerging **issue** are:

- Will the **issue**(s) affect the organisation's bottom line in any way?
- When is the **issue** likely to impact on the organisation?
- Can organisational action change the likely outcome of the **issue**?
- According to the organisation's analyses of the above questions, are their current practices and policies correct?
- Does the organisation have the **resources** and will to work on the **issue**(s) at present?
- What are the financial or policy **benefits** for the organisation in dealing with the **issue**(s)?
- What can the organisation learn to its benefit from dealing with the **issue**(s)?
- How can the organisation evaluate the effectiveness of its actions in dealing with the **issue**(s)?
- What can the organisation learn from the situation to ensure that it remains competitive in the future?

Because the evolution of an **issue** often results in changes in policy, the earlier an **issue** can be identified and managed, the easier it is for an organisation to resolve conflict and minimise any cost implications or damage to its reputation. Meng (1987) identified six possible groups or **publics** which make **issue**s:

- associates
- employee associations
- the general public
- the Government
- the media
- special or general interest groups

An **issue** begins as an idea which may have a potential impact on an organisation or set of publics. This in turn may result in an action which brings increased awareness or a reaction. Hainsworth (1990) and Meng (1992) claim that this process is cyclical and is made up of four stages: origin, mediation and amplification, organisation and resolution. In Figure 9 the vertical axis of the diagram represents the level of pressure exerted on an organisation by a developing **issue**; the horizontal axis represents the various stages of development. At each stage of the model, pressure mounts on the organisation to respond in order to prevent a **crisis**.

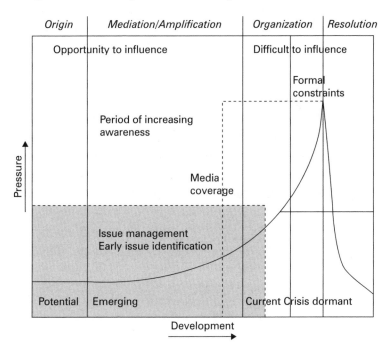

Figure 9 Hainsworth and Meng's model of the issue life cycle

Chase, W. H. and Jones, B. L. (1979) 'Managing public policy issues', *Public Relations Review*, Summer.

Hainsworth, B. (1990) 'Issues management: An overview', *Public Relations Review*, 16, 1.

Meng, M. B. (1987) 'Issues management today', unpub. thesis, Bingham Young University,

Meng, M. B. (1992) 'Early identification aids issues management', *Public Relations Journal*, Mar.

Regester, M. and Larkin, J. (2005) *Risk Issues and Crisis Management*, 3rd edn. London: Kogan Page.

I

Jingle

A jingle is a memorable **slogan**, set to an appealing melody and broadcast on radio and television advertisements.

Johari window

A Johari window is a psychological **tool** created by Joseph Luft and Harry Ingham in 1955 to help people understand their **interpersonal communication** (see Figure 10). It is used in **public relations** in corporate settings to measure interpersonal effectiveness. When performing the exercise, the subject is given a list of fifty-five adjectives and picks four or five which they feel best describe their personality. Peers are also asked to repeat the procedure, picking four or five adjectives which best describe the subject. These are then mapped on to a grid.

Adjectives selected by both parties are placed in the arena quadrant. This represents **traits** that both parties are aware the subject possesses.

Adjectives which are chosen only by the subject and not by his or her peers are placed in the façade quadrant. This represents information about the subject of which the peers are unaware. It is then up to the subject to disclose the information or not.

Adjectives chosen by the peers but not the subject are placed in the blind spot quadrant. These represent information of which the peers are aware but the subject is not. It is then up to the peers to disclose the information or not.

Adjectives not selected by either party remain in the unknown quadrant, representing those motives and behaviours not recognised by anyone. This may be because they do not apply or because there is a collective ignorance of the **trait**.

Luft, J. and Ingham, H. (1955) 'The Johari Window: A graphic model for interpersonal awareness', *Proceedings of the Western Training Laboratory in Group Development*. Los Angeles, CA: UCLA.

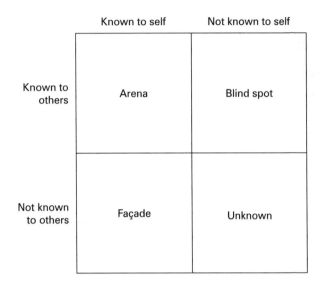

Figure 10   An empty Johari window

Journalist

A journalist gathers and disseminates information about current events, **trends**, **issue**s and people. Journalists are the **gatekeepers** of information and the recipients of a **public relations** practitioner's **press release**s. The relationship between journalists and **public relations** practitioners is one fraught with ambiguity and can often be adversarial. The relationship depends on the **public relations** practitioner providing journalists with information they consider to be in the public interest and, most of all, newsworthy. It also needs to be presented in a format which is acceptable. The job of the **public relations** officer is to build trusting relationships with journalists in order to keep open the communication channels with the **publics**. Journalists need the news stories and the **public relations** practitioners can provide them. Center and Jackson (2003) suggest a simple list of **media relations** guidelines to ease the process:

1 Begin with a sound knowledge of how to gather news stories and evaluate them. Put them in the best format for disseminating to either broadcast or print.
2 Make sure that the organisation has a designated spokesperson at short notice.

3 Make sure that the spokesperson practises **transparency** and is candid in response to enquiries, bearing in mind security **issue**s and compassionate consideration.
4 Continuously educate and train employees on how to handle themselves in media situations.
5 Be prepared for the unexpected. Have a **crisis management** plan in hand.

A journalist may practise several types of journalism including:

- *broadcast*: television, radio;
- *on-line (cyber)*: World Wide Web, internet;
- *sports*: all sports-related topics;
- *science*: all science-related topics;
- *investigative*: the exposure of unethical, immoral and illegal behaviour;
- *new*: conversational speech, first-person narratives, telling story using 'scenes';
- *gonzo*: punchy style, rough language, disregard for conventional journalistic practices;
- *celebrity*: personal lives of celebrities and other famous people;
- *convergence*: the combination of print and photographic and video;
- *ambush*: aggressive **tactics** to confront people;
- *gotcha*: unethical reporting which manipulates facts to portray a person or organisation in a particular way.

Center, A. H. and Jackson, P. (2003) *Public Relations Practices*, 6th edn. Englewood Cliffs, NJ: Prentice Hall.

J

Key words and phrases

Key words and phrases relate to the essential message of a communication. These key words or phrases are often given a prominent position or repeated in communications such as **advertisements** or **speeches**. The fact that they are repetitive and memorable means that they often have a subliminal impact upon the targeted recipient – even if the rest of the **message** is forgotten.

See **rhetoric, speech-writing/speech-making.**

KISS principle

KISS stands for <u>K</u>eep <u>I</u>t <u>S</u>imple <u>S</u>tupid. It is an acronym often used by **copywriters** and **public relations** writers who promote the concept of clear, uncluttered writing to create effective communication.

Knowledge and understanding

Public relations has a vital part to play in helping to inform the general public and its own **stakeholders** by providing information in a comprehensible and accessible format in order to prevent ignorance of a product or service through knowledge and understanding.

Landscaping

Landscaping is another term for a targeted media list, often associated with **grassroots** communication.

Laswell (Harold)

Harold Lasswell (1902–1978) was a leading American political scientist and communications theorist who argued that democracies needed **propaganda** to keep the uninformed citizenry in agreement with what the **dominant coalition** had determined was in their best interests. In 1948 he shaped a formula to explain the communication process:

Who (says) What (to) Whom (in) What Channel (with) What Effect?

However, this **communication model** assumes that communication will always have an effect and suggests that communication is always persuasive. It is most suited to the **propaganda** model of communication.

Latent publics

Latent publics have been defined by James **Grunig**, as groups of people or **stakeholders** who face a problem as a result of an organisation's actions, but fail to recognise the problem. For example, a local factory may be expanding its business and in turn may be increasing its pollution output, but the local community may be unaware of this.

See **Grunig (James), publics.**

Law of primacy and recency (in persuasion)

In 1925, Lund's 'law of primacy in persuasion' as applied to public communications held that the side of an **issue** presented first holds more sway and is more effective than the side presented subsequently. Lund gave his classes of college students a mimeographed communication in support of one side of a controversial **issue** and then presented a second communication advocating the opposite stand on the same **issue**. He discovered that the first communication influenced the students more than the second. However, subsequent experiments gave different results. Cromwell (1950) did a study where affirmative and negative speeches were presented to a group of students whose opinions were measured before and after. He found a significant 'recency' effect in favour of the side of the **issue** presented last. To explain the contradictory results, Hovland and Mandell (1957) replicated the Lund experiment. Their results indicated more recency effects than primary. As these studies used written communication, Hovland and his associates concluded that when two sides of an **issue** are presented successfully by different communicators, the side presented first does not necessarily have the advantage. Further experiments concluded that if after hearing only one side of a controversial argument, the opinion is expressed publicly in favour of that, the effectiveness of the second side is reduced, leading to a primacy effect.

Cromwell, H. (1950) 'The relative effect on audience attitude of the first versus the second argumentative speech of a series', *Speech Monog.*, 17 105–122.

Hovland, C. I. and Mandell, W. (1957) *Yale Studies in Attitude and Communications*, Vol. 1, The Order of Presentation in Persuasion. New Haven, CT: Yale University Press.

Lund, F. H. (1925) The psychology of belief iv: The law of primacy in persuasion, *Journal of Abnormal Social Psychology*, 20, 183–191.

Lead time

Lead time is the publishing term for describing the amount of time that a **journalist** has between receiving a writing assignment and submitting the completed piece. Lead times differ depending on the type of publication, from a few hours to several months. Lead times are an important consideration for **public relations** practitioners when **pitch**ing a story or sending a **press release** to **journalist**s.

Leading questions

Leading questions are used to elicit and influence a required response. Questions can be asked which persuade respondents to offer answers at odds with their real perceptions or experiences. There are four main types of leading question:

1 *Conversational leads*: these occur in everyday conversation, e.g. 'Have you ever seen a more lovely morning?'
2 *Simple leads*: a tag question, e.g. 'You don't buy this product do you?' acts as a simple lead in order to favour a particular response.
3 *Implication leads*: this works by giving the choice of either going along with the lead or accepting a negative implication embedded in the question, e.g. 'Do I understand that like all responsible people you would never buy a product from this company?'
4 *Subtle leads*: bias can be introduced into questioning in a subtle manner by framing the question in a particular way, e.g. instead of asking 'How long was the film?', the questioner may ask, 'How short was the film?'

See **interpersonal communication, questionnaires.**

Hargie, O. (2006) *The Handbook of Communication Skills*. London: Routledge.

Leapfrog effect

See **product/service life cycle (activities of public relations).**

Lee (Ivy)

Ivy Ledbetter Lee (1877–1934), along with Edward **Bernays**, is considered by some to be the father of **public relations**, and is certainly one of the pioneers of modern **public relations**. Lee evolved his philosophy of **public relations** in 1906 into the *Declaration of Principles,* the first articulation of the concept that **public relations** practitioners have a public responsibility which extends beyond the needs of the client. In the same year, after an accident with the Pennsylvania Railroad, Lee issued what is considered the first **press release**, convincing the company to be transparent and openly disclose details of the accident before **journalist**s heard them elsewhere. In 1912 he was hired by the railroad as an executive-level **public relations** communicator. In 1919 he founded the **public relations** counselling office, Ivy Lee and Associates, serving the Rockefellers and their corporate interests. He taught the first

L

public relations course at New York University in 1912 where he remained a tutor for a decade. Lee became an inaugural member of the Council for Foreign Relations in the United States in 1921. Although Lee espoused the use of **two-way communication**, he often practised **propaganda** methods and just before his death he had been investigated by the US Congress for his work in Nazi Germany on behalf of the company IG Farben.

Hiebert, R. E. (1966) *Courtier to the Crowd: The Story of Ivy Lee and the Development of Public Relations*. Ames: Iowa State University Press.

Libel

See **defamation.**

Likert scale

A Likert scale is a form of psychometric response scale found in **questionnaires** and is widely used in survey **research**. Respondents specify their level of agreement to a given statement and tick a corresponding number. There are seven- and nine-point scales but traditionally a five-point scale is used:

1 Strongly disagree
2 Disagree
3 Neither disagree nor agree
4 Agree
5 Strongly disagree.

Responses to a single Likert item are treated as ordinal data, because the **research**er cannot assume that each respondent perceives the difference between levels as equidistant. This ordinal data can then be collated on to bar charts.

Likert, R. (1932) A technique for measurement of attitudes, *Archives of Psychology*, 140, 1–55.

L

Lobbying

One of the **techniques** commonly used in **issues management** is lobbying. Lobbying involves direct attempts to influence legislative and regulatory decisions in government. Organisations have increasingly used lobbying **techniques** to present their case to government and groups of **stakeholders**. Lobbying can be either defensive (designed to abolish or amend an existing law) or offensive (aimed at pushing the government to create a new law). Organisations which wish to lobby may use an in-house specialist. This is most likely to succeed as an in-house specialist will have an in-depth knowledge of the organisation and its position. Alternatively, a specialist consultancy may be hired on an ad hoc basis. Some organisations, notably charities, retain MPs or peers to provide them with advice and the means of access to government decision-makers. However, recent cases of questionable behaviour by MPs, parliamentary lobbyists and government press advisers have caused concern, and calls have been made for better regulation in the UK. The public perception of an **issue** will increase in proportion to the amount of media coverage it receives. The public agenda then influences the political agenda, as politicians seek to respond to what they think voters want in order to secure their own positions.

There are several methods which MPs can use to further the causes of lobbyists. MPs ask over fifty thousand Parliamentary Questions (PQs) each year. Questions are printed on the order paper on the day they are tabled at the table office and again on the day they are answered. All questions and answers appear in Hansard. MPs can also put down an Early Day Motion (EDM) on the order paper to call the House, government or an individual MP to take action. MPs also have the opportunity to effect policy by working in party committees or departmental groups.

Roche (1998) suggests that the following factors are necessary for successful lobbying:

- access to decision-makers
- background **research**
- good timing
- excellent communication skills
- knowledge of government procedure
- public interest
- support of opinion leaders
- effective targeting
- favourable media coverage
- knowledge of government structure.

L

Roche, K. (1998) 'Lobbying', unpublished dissertation thesis, Leeds Metropolitan University.

Souza, C. (1998) *So You Want to Be a Lobbyist? The Inside Story of the Political Lobbying Industry*. London: Politico's.

Logo

A logo is a symbol, emblem, icon, **ideogram** or sign which forms a unique trademark or commercial **brand** and is part of an organisation's **corporate identity**. A logo should be immediately recognisable and inspire trust, admiration and loyalty. Logos are used to identify organisations and should be able to 'stand alone' without any text to make the commercial **brand** familiar. The use of colour is important in logo design and **brand** recognition, but should not conflict with the functionality of the logo. For example, loud colours such as red are often used to convey danger signals on the roads, green is often associated with health food and products. Because logos are used to foster immediate customer recognition they should not be changed or redesigned frequently. Well-known examples of effective logos include the Red Cross, Apple, Coca-Cola; IBM, Pepsi, McDonald's, BMW, Mercedez-Benz, Nike and Adidas.

Longitudinal research

Longitudinal research measures changes in trends over a period of time and can be represented in the form of graphs, bar charts and pie charts. Longitudinal research is particularly useful in **public relations**, especially when measuring how perceptions of an organisation and its services or products have changed during the time of an extended **public relations campaign**.

L

Mm

Macnamara's model of evaluation

Evaluation is an important part of the planning process and one often overlooked by **public relations** practitioners. Jim Macnamara designed a useful model to make this process clearer (see Table 5). The model is divided into stages: results, outputs and inputs and also identifies associated activities and **evaluation** methodologies in which the practitioner can engage. The model needs to be customised for each project but the basics remain the same.

Mailing lists

Mailing lists are up-to-date lists, usually held electronically, of media contacts. They are used to target **messages** to the appropriate media.

Market research

Market research is the systematic process of gathering information about an organisation's customers and competitors and the market. Market research is used in **public relations planning**, for the launch of new products and services, for the expansion and improvement of existing products and services and for the expansion into new markets.

See **demographics, segmentation.**

Kolb, B. (2008) *Marketing Research, a Practical Approach*. London: Sage.
Stone, M. A. and Desmond J. (2007) *Fundamentals of Marketing*. Abingdon: Routledge.

Marketing

Marketing is the field most commonly confused with **public relations**, often because marketing refers to **public relations** in its texts and practice as part of the **marketing mix**. The Chartered

M

Table 5 Evaluation based on Macnamara's model

Stage	Activities	Methodologies
Results	Objective achieved or problem solved	**Observation** Quantitative **research**
	Number who behave in a desired manner	Sales statistics, enrolments Quantitative **research** Qualitative **research** (cognition acceptance)
	Number who change **attitudes**	Qualitative **research**: readership, listenership, viewing statistics Attendance at events Inquiry or response rates (e.g. coupons, calls)
	Number who learn message content (e.g. increased knowledge, awareness, understanding)	Circulation figures **Audience analysis**
	Number who consider **messages**	Circulation figures **Audience analysis**

	Number who receive **messages**	**Analysis** of media coverage (**content analysis**)	**Audience** surveys Awards
Outputs	Number of **messages** supporting **objectives**	**Media monitoring** (clippings and **broadcast media** tapes) Distribution statistics	Review Pre-testing (e.g. **focus groups**)
	Number of **messages** placed in the media	**Media monitoring** Distribution statistics	Review Pre-testing
	Number of **messages** sent	Expert review **Feedback**	
	Quality of message presentation (e.g. **newsletter** or brochure design, newsworthiness of story)	Readability tests (e.g. Gunning, Flesch, SST)	
Inputs	Appropriateness of message content	Readability tests	
	Appropriateness of medium	**Case studies** Pre-testing	
	Adequacy of background information, intelligence, **research**	Review	Benchmark

M

Institute of Marketing defines marketing as the 'management process responsible for identifying, anticipating and satisfying consumer requirements profitably'. The most important words here are consumer and profit – there is a clear exchange of money for goods or services.

Marketing is easily measured and marketing campaigns are preceded by in-depth **research** into consumer demands and needs. Marketing clearly differs from **public relations** which exists to maintain and protect reputations and to create understanding between an organisation and its **publics**.

Sutherland, J. and Canwell, D. (2007) *Key Concepts in Marketing*. Basingstoke: Palgrave Macmillan.
www.cim.co.uk

Marketing communications

Marketing communications are across-the-board communications designed to help move a potential customer from a state of ignorance to a position of decision, desire and action. Norman Hart (1995) describes the adoption process set out below:

1 *Awareness*: the individual becomes aware of the innovation but lacks information about it.
2 *Interest*: the individual is stimulated to seek information about the innovation.
3 **Evaluation**: the individual considers whether it would make sense to try the innovation.
4 *Trial*: the individual tries the innovation on a small scale to improve his/her estimation of its utility.
5 *Adoption*: the individual decides to make full and regular use of the innovation.

M

Marketing communications, therefore, consist of any form of communication which helps to convert a non-customer to a customer, and subsequently retains that custom. **Public relations** contributes most to the **promotion**al element of the **marketing mix**; the media and **messages** used to influence buyer decisions. It is here that **public relations** supports and supplements **advertising** and **marketing**.

See **marketing, marketing public relations.**

Hart, Norman (1995) *Strategic Public Relations*. London: Macmillan Business Press.
Kotler, P., Armstrong, G., Saunders, J. and Wong, V. (2001) *Principles of Marketing: European Edition*, London: *Financial Times*, Englewood Cliffs, NJ: Prentice-Hall.

Marketing mix

The **four Ps** of **marketing** are known as the marketing mix (see Figure 11):

1 *Product*: product refers to the actual physical product or service offered to the consumer.
2 *Price*: price refers to the list price of the product or service.
3 *Place*: refers to the channels of distribution needed to get the product to market.
4 ***Promotion***: refers to the **promotion**al and communication elements of selling to potential customers.

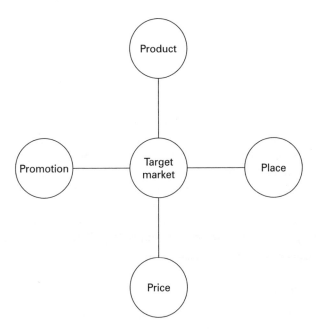

Figure 11   The marketing mix

Marketing managers need to control and blend these variables in order to satisfy customers in the target market. Aspects of the 4 Ps are shown in Table 6.

Marketing public relations (MPR)

MPR relates to the direct merging of **marketing** and **public relations** and is based around an organisation's dealings with consumers

Table 6   Aspects of the 4 Ps

Product	Price	Place	Promotion
Functionality	List price	Channels of distribution	**Advertising**
Appearance	Discounts	Market coverage	**Public relations**
Quality	Financing	Locations	Personal selling
Brand	Leasing options	Logistics	Message
Packaging		Service levels	Media
Warranty			**Budget**
Service and support			

regarding **marketing** matters. MPR is usually effective in areas which may originally have been served by **advertising** and **brand** building, such as cultivating new customers, introducing new products and influencing **opinion formers and leaders.** The disciplines of **marketing** and **public relations** are moving ever closer together as MPR concerns itself with corporate advertising, media **strategy** and surveys into employee **attitudes** and customer satisfaction, and **public relations** takes responsibility for news, **community relations**, **lobbying** and **corporate social responsibility** and investments.

See **marketing, marketing communications.**

Mass media

Mass media is used to denote media especially designed to reach a mass or very large **audience**. It includes television, radio, newspapers, magazines and books, the internet, personal web pages, **blog**s and **podcast**s.

Media analysis

See **content analysis.**

Media effects

Mass communication involves the scientific study of the **mass media**, the **messages** they generate, the **audience**s they try to reach and their effects on these **audience**s. Media effects generally include any of the psychological or sociological outcomes following **mass media** exposure or consumption and refers to theories about the ways in which the **mass media** affect how their **audience**s think and behave. The media has a strong social and cultural impact upon society and the shift towards new media technology has caused some media theorists to challenge the influence that the media have over **attitudes** and **beliefs**.

See **hypodermic needle model, uses and gratifications.**

Curran, J. and Seaton, J. (2002) *Power without Responsibility: The Press, Broadcasting and New Media in Britain,* 6th edn. London: Routledge.

Media monitoring

Media **attitudes** are measured and monitored by analysing the **press clippings** or **scripts** from broadcast monitors. Monitoring analyses:

- what the media are saying about the organisation (if anything);
- what the quality of the coverage is;
- whether the media are reporting correctly;
- whether the media are critical or sympathetic;
- what sort of press coverage any competitors are receiving.

See **content analysis.**

Media planning

Public relations practitioners engage in the process of media planning when **research**ing which media to target for their **public relations** communications and **messages**. There are a number of notable media directories to aid this process, such as **BRAD, Benns Media Directory** and **Willings Press Guide**.

Katz, H. (2007) *The Media Handbook: A Complete Guide to Advertising, Media Selection, Planning, Research and Buying,* 3rd edn. Mahwah, NY: Lawrence Erlbaum.

M

Media relations

The media are the **gatekeeper**s of information and as such are a vital resource for **public relations** practitioners, notably for their role in forming **public opinion**. The branch of **public relations** aimed at making and retaining the relationship between an organisation and the media is termed 'media relations'.

It is usually the function of the press office to engage in and manage media relations. Although entitled the press office, **press officer**s communicate with all types of media, not just the press. The **press officer** has two main responsibilities: to initiate media coverage and to supply information on demand by the media. The role is both reactive and proactive and is based on **two-way communication**. Media relations involves targeting the **gatekeeper**s of the mass and specialised media for communication about the client or organisation through a process known as **media planning.** However, the ultimate targeted **audience** of media relations are the consumers of the media.

Media relations is largely tactical in nature and can contribute to the organisation's longer-term strategic **objectives**, such as:

- improving the company or brand image;
- gaining a higher and better media profile;
- changing the **attitudes** of the target **audience**;
- improving relationships with the community;
- increasing market share;
- influencing government policy at local, national or international level;
- improving communications with investors and their advisers;
- improving **industrial relations**.

The **public relations** practitioner has a number of tasks to perform in relation to the media. These include:

- finding information on the media and maintaining files and information (**media planning** and **media scanning**);
- co-ordinating **editorial** schedules of relevant media;
- maintaining up-to-date media contacts through personal liaison;
- **research**ing specialist freelance contacts;
- exploring new channels of communication and their relevance to **public relations**.

Of paramount importance to media relations is the news or **press release**. Other tactical media relations **tools** include:

- **press conference**s or **press receptions**
- virtual **press conference**s
- informal media briefings
- exclusive and other **media interviews**
- media tours
- **facility visits**
- **on-line press** offices
- photo calls

M

- **television** and **radio advertisements**
- features and **articles**
- **vlogs**, **blog**s, **website**s and **podcast**s.

See **gatekeeper, journalist.**

Bland, M., Theaker, A. and Wragg, D. (2005) *Effective Media Relations, How to Get Results*, 3rd edn. London: Kogan Page.

Media review

See **media scanning.**

Media scanning

Public relations practitioners engage in media scanning or reviewing as a process of **evaluation** in order to see what **journalist**s have previously said about their client or organisation. It involves scanning newspapers, **articles**, **website**s and **broadcast media** and engaging in **content analysis**. The process of media scanning usually precedes **media planning** and is part of the **research** process of a media or **public relations campaign**. There are several questions a **public relations** practitioner should be asking within the review, such as:

1 How is the problem defined?
2 What solutions, if any, are given?
3 Who is identified as responsible for creating the problem?
4 Who is held accountable for solving the problem?
5 Is the problem portrayed as the plight of the individual or the problem of a larger group or of society in general?
6 What is being said?
7 What is being left out and therefore marginalised or portrayed as less important?
8 What images (if any) are used to cover the story?
9 Who is the **journalist** whose opinions are deemed valid?

See **media planning, research.**

Messages

The nature of messages will vary with the nature of the **public relations programme/plan** or campaign and the nature of the **audience**. Every **public relations** campaign needs a firm set of messages to form the mainstay of the communication. These messages

M

must be clear and easily understandable as they are the point of contact between an organisation and its **publics** in communication terms. Anne **Gregory** (2004) suggests that there are four steps in determining messages:

1 take existing articulated perceptions;
2 define what shifts can be made in those perceptions;
3 identify elements of **persuasion**;
4 ensure that the messages are credible and deliverable through **public relations**.

The integrity of the message is affected by many **issue**s which determine whether it is taken seriously or not, these being format, tone, context, timing and repetition.

Gregory, A. (2004) *Planning and Managing Public Relations Campaigns.* London: Kogan Page.

Mexican statement

At the first World Assembly of Public Relations Associations held in Mexico City in December 1978, the following definition of the nature and purpose of **public relations** was unanimously adopted: 'Public relations practice is the art and social science of analysing trends, predicting their consequences, counselling organizations' leaders and implementing planned programmes of action which will serve both the organization and the public interest.'

See **public relations.**

Micro media

Not all **public relations** media are addressed to the mass public (macro media). It is often more effective for **public relations messages** to be addressed directly to small groups or **face-to-face communication** with individuals. This is termed micro media and can include specially created media such as audio and video CDs and **DVDs**, slides, notice boards, internal and external **house journals**, private **exhibitions**, seminars, **conferences**, educational literature, **sponsorships** and books.

Mintel

Mintel is a global supplier of consumer media and **market research**. Mintel helps **research**ers discover opportunities, monitor competition, develop products and services, and hone **marketing, advertising** and **public relations** efforts.

See **Ipsos MORI, secondary research.**

www.mintel.com

Mission statement

A mission statement is a short statement of the purpose of a company or organisation. It is intended to provide direction. Everyone involved in the organisation should be aware of the mission statement and what it means. A mission statement should serve as a standard against which to measure actions. It should be simple, clear and direct and should answer the following three basic questions:

1 What are the opportunities or needs that we exist to address (the *purpose* of the organisation)?
2 What are we doing to address these needs (the *business* of the organisation)?
3 What principles of **beliefs** guide our work (the ***values*** of the organisation)?

For example, Google's mission statement is to 'organise the world's information and make it universally accessible and useful'. Mission statements are sometimes used as **advertising slogans**.

Haschak, P. (1998) *Corporate Statements: The Official Missions, Goals, Principles and Philosophies of over 900 Companies*. Jefferson, NC: McFarland.

Motivating sequence

A motivating sequence is a copy formula for creating **advertisements** and other types of **promotion**al and **public relations** copy. They include the **AIDA model**, **the BFD Formula**, **ACCA** and the **Four Ps**.

Mutual understanding

To gain mutual understanding should be the aim of every **public relations** campaign and message. It is concerned with understanding the organisation's **publics** and facilitating their understanding of the organisation by managing relationships with them.

See **knowledge and understanding.**

M

N n

Nash equilibrium model

See **game theory, win–win.**

Negotiation

Negotiation is a process between two or more people designed to resolve disputes and agree upon a course of action, hopefully leading to a **win–win** situation.

Netiquette

Netiquette refers to the 'etiquette of cyber-space'. All **public relations** practitioners should become ethnographers and study the culture of electronic mail so as not to be accidentally offensive in their communications. This is especially important when interviewing electronically.

Networking

Networking refers to the process of forming mutually beneficial and supportive relationships with like-minded individuals. These connections and social contacts may help in the **public relations** and communication processes of the organisation.

News agencies

See **external media support.**

News conference

The essential element of a news or **press conference** is that it must be for the purpose of disseminating 'newsworthy' news, be it good or bad, which is of consequence or interest to the wider public. It is a media **event** and a **public relations** platform for the organisation. Press events facilitate dialogue with **journalists** because reporters can probe and question. They can also set the agenda for their own stories. The main objective of the news conference is to make an announcement to the public via the media which enables the audience to perceive the news in a positive light. The **public relations** practitioner has a number of **issues** to consider when planning, organising and managing a news conference, such as:

- choosing the venue and time;
- sending out **press releases/news releases**;
- inviting selected **journalists**;
- deciding on the tone and intent of **messages**;
- designing and writing **press packs** and other forms of written communication;
- writing the speeches;
- managing audio and **visual communications, photo opportunities**, etc;
- setting up a press room for **journalists**;
- planning the seating arrangements;
- proactively planning a list of possible questions from **journalists** with appropriate responses from the speakers;
- organising **hospitality** for **journalists**;
- evaluating and reviewing post-conference;
- carrying out **media analysis**.

Leinemann, R. and Baikaltseva, E. (2006) *How to Manage a Successful Press Conference*. Aldershot: Gower.

News release

See **press release.**

N

News pyramid

The news pyramid is a method used for writing **feature articles** and **newsletters**. The writer should begin the story with the most important **issues** and work downwards towards the base of the pyramid (see Figure 12).

The double pyramid, sometimes called the Wall Street Journal method, has a small pyramid on top of a larger one (See Figure 13). Instead of starting with the most important point, the writer gives

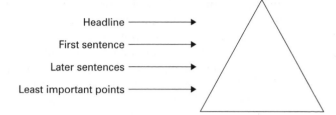

Figure 12   Layout of a single pyramid story

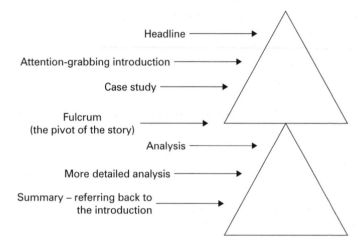

Figure 13   The double pyramid method

a vignette or case study (see **case studies**), often about a person. This story is then amplified, extended, explained and justified until the reader learns the 'meat' of the story. This method seduces the reader into learning about a major **issue** by taking a human angle or by looking at one small aspect of the **issue**. The double pyramid is appropriate for relaxed, analytical **articles**, rather than urgent, front-page stories.

Newsgroups

Newsgroups are groups of people who share common interests and who communicate on-line. They can be a powerful **research tool** for the **public relations** practitioner. Newsgroups can be monitored for content and used as a central place to garner information and as a forum to recruit new respondents for a **research** study. They can also serve as an area to collect creative ideas and to obtain information about the competition.

Newsletter

A newsletter or **house journal** is the company's mouthpiece and can be used as part of both internal and external **public relations** and communications. Organisations use newsletters as an effective method of informing their employees and customers of what they are doing. As internal and external relationships differ, most organisations have separate publications for communicating with differing **audience**s. The employee publication is a newsletter designed principally for an internal **audience**, while industrial and company publications are usually associated with vehicles packaged primarily for external **audience**s. Trade publications are aimed at professionals in a specific area of manufacturing or service. Because newsletters are a **controlled media**, **public relations** professionals can say and write what they like; there is no **gatekeeper** to monitor output. This means that the writer has more control over the quality and the content of the writing and therefore more control over accomplishing message-acceptance **objectives**. Newsletters are an effective **tool** for communicating **messages** to people which put the organisation on the public's agenda, but because members of the public often have no strong reason to consume one of these newsletters, they cannot be expected to form or change cognitions, **attitudes** and behaviours.

Many newsletters contain some or all of the following items:

- the organisation's plan;
- personnel policies;
- productivity improvements;
- job-related information;
- job-advancement opportunities;
- the effect of external events on jobs;
- the organisation's competitive position;
- news about other departments/divisions;
- how individual jobs fit into the overall organisation;
- how the organisation uses profits;
- personal news and views.

Non-profit public relations

Public relations is the key to survival for non-profit organisations (including charities, schools, churches, art galleries, museums,

N

voluntary organisations, etc). **Public relations** is essential for **fund-raising**, attracting members and energising and maintaining supporters and for fulfilling the organisation's **mission**, aims and **objectives**. Although **non-profit public relations** has many things in common with **public relations** for the profit sector, there are some fundamental differences. Non-profits are often involved in 'worthy' causes and as such are engaged in fulfilling a significant mission as opposed to increasing a corporate bottom line. They often have difficulties in getting their **messages** heard – especially if they are working for an 'unpopular' cause such as prison reform or aid for asylum seekers. They also have fewer **resources** and so have to be persistent and innovative when **pitch**ing stories to the media. A public relations campaign or plan will need to be followed, taking into account the logical planning process, regardless of whether the organisation is for profit or not.

Feinglass, A. (2005) *The Public Relations Handbook for Nonprofits: A Comprehensive and Practical Guide*. San Francisco, CA: Jossey-Bass.

Radtke, J. M. (1998) *Strategic Communication for Nonprofit Organisations: Seven Steps to Creating a Successful Plan*. New York: Wiley.

Non-publics

Non-publics fall into one of the categories of **publics** defined by James **Grunig.** They are groups of people who are neither affected by nor affect an organisation because it has no relevance to them. This group of publics often remains unidentified and is ignored in **public relations** campaigns.

See **Grunig (James), publics**

N

Objectives

Setting realistic and achievable objectives is vital when planning the **public relations programme/plan**. Objectives form the direction and destination of the programme and can be used to evaluate and measure achievement. Before the planning stage even begins, the **public relations** practitioner must consider the following questions:

- What should the **public relations programme/plan** achieve?
- Does the organisation have the means of coping with and managing these objectives?
- What is the timescale for the programme?

Anne **Gregory** (2004) suggests that objectives are usually set at one of three levels:

- *Awareness objectives*: getting the target **publics** to think about something and trying to promote a level of understanding. Awareness objectives are also referred to as cognitive objectives.
- *Attitude and opinion objectives*: getting the target **publics** to form a certain **attitude** or opinion about an object or **issue**. **Attitude** and opinion objectives are also referred to as affective objectives.
- *Behaviour objectives*: getting the target **publics** to behave in a desired way. Behaviour objectives are also referred to as conative objectives.

It is more problematic to get individuals to act than it is to get them to think about something, so most **public relations** objectives will be set at the cognitive and affective levels rather than at the conative. Consequently, a **public relations programme/plan** might have the following objectives:

- to create awareness;
- to promote understanding;

- to overcome misunderstanding or apathy;
- to inform;
- to develop knowledge;
- to displace prejudice;
- to encourage **belief**;
- to confirm or realign a perception;
- to act in a particular way.

It is generally accepted that the objectives should be **SMART**.

See **attitudes, beliefs, values.**

Gregory, A. (2004) *Planning and Managing a Public Relations Campaign.* London: Kogan Page.

Observation

Observation is a **research** methodology which requires careful planning and piloting. It is a technique which can reveal characteristics of groups or individuals which would have been impossible to discover by other means. There are two main types of observation – *participant* and *non-participant*. Participant observation involves **research**ers immersing themselves mentally, physically and emotionally into a new group setting. They have no preconceived ideas and no checklists or charts. They observe events, situations and behaviours and write up their results immediately. However, the limitations presented have obvious problems with regard to interpretation and subjectivity. Unstructured observation is time-consuming but can be useful to generate hypotheses. Non-participants faithfully record their observations, usually using video or audio recording, and then interpret the data. Grids, schedules and checklists can all be used to structure observation (see Table 7).

O

Table 7   Observation checklist

Primary areas	Secondary areas
Decide exactly what information is needed.	List all topics/aspects about which information is requzired.
Consider why this information is needed.	Examine the list and remove any item not directly associated with the task in hand.
Decide if observation is the most efficacious methodology.	Consider alternatives.

(Continued)

Table 7 Continued

Primary areas	Secondary areas
Decide which aspects are necessary to investigate.	Decide if content, process, interaction or intervention is most interesting.
Request permission.	Clear official channels.
Devise a suitable checklist, grid or chart.	Consult published examples and adapt if necessary.
Consider what will be done with the information.	Will the data produced be sufficient to enable conclusions?
Pilot the method and revise if necessary.	Memorise categories. Devise short-hand symbols. Practise.
Prepare before observation.	Plan the room layout and seating arrangements. Prepare grids etc.
Decide where to sit (as observer).	Be unobtrusive.
Remember that no grid will tell the complete 'story'.	Place the event in its organisational context.
Analyse and interpret the data.	Consider the implications of the facts.
Thank the participants involved.	

Source: Adapted from Bell (1999).

Bell, J. (1999) *Doing Your Research Project*, 3rd edn. Buckingham: Open University Press.

O

On-line copywriting assignments

The actual deliverables in on-line **copywriting** can be hard to iden-tify. **Copywriter** Robert Bly (2005) suggests the following as the most typical on-line copywriting assignments for **public relations** practitioners, marketers and **copywriter**s.

A microsite, also known as a long-copy landing stage, is a **web-site** designed to sell a product such as a **newsletter**, e-book or e-presentation. Microsites are generally equivalent to a sales letter of between four and eight pages.

A short-copy landing page is simply a landing page for a prod-uct or offer and is often used for **white paper**s and software demonstrations. They are generally the same length as a magazine advertisement with a headline, a few paragraphs of product description in the **body copy** and an on-line order form.

A transaction page is similar to a short-copy landing page but with less product description. It is a basic on-line form that the visitor can use to request more information or order the product.

A long-copy e-mail is designed to sell the product directly by driving the reader to the short-copy landing page or the transaction page.

A teaser e-mail is a short e-mail designed to drive readers to a microsite or long-copy landing page where they can order the product and it is generally the on-line equivalent of a half-page to two-page sales letter.

A lead-generation e-mail is similar to the teaser e-mail but its purpose is to drive visitors to the landing or transaction page where they can request a free white paper or other information.

An on-line e-mail conversion series consists of a series of follow-up e-mails sent by autoresponder and designed to convert the enquiry into an actual sale.

An on-line advertisement is generally a 100-word classified ad which runs in an **e-zine**.

A pop-under is a window which appears on a **website**, typically when the visitor leaves without ordering. Pop-unders make a special offer in exchange for the visitor's e-mail details.

See **copywriting, white paper.**

Bly, R. W. (2005) *The Copywriter's Handbook: A Step-by-Step Guide to Writing Copy that Sells*, 3rd edn. New York: Henry Holt.

On-line press

The increase in the use of the internet has led to huge changes in the way in which readers interact with the news media, and pressure to grow and expand has led to the need for newspapers to compete internationally. Most newspapers and many magazines now have on-line versions and **journalist**s have to duplicate their efforts to manage both paper press and on-line press. **Public relations** practitioners also have to learn to deal with the different deadlines and agendas of a more diverse range of media.

Temple, N. (2003) *Writing Copy for the Web in a Week*. London: Hodder and Stoughton.

On-line research techniques

On-line **research** is an important t**ool** for the **public relations** practitioner. It is quick, easy and inexpensive compared with other traditional **research** methods. It offers a viable way to facilitate **interviews**, conduct **surveys** and monitor **public opinion**. Although the internet offers a plethora of **research** possibilities, it still has its limitations, notably the fact that not all individuals have access to the new technology. On-line **research** methods include the use of the internet and **intranet**, on-line interviewing, e-mail surveys, **web surveys**, **focus groups** and **newsgroups**.

See **qualitative research methods, quantitative research methods, research.**

Open questions

Open questions invite respondents to address a particular topic. Open questions are sometimes referred to as 'unquestions' because they frequently begin with words such as 'why' and 'what'. Open questions are broad in nature and require more than one or two words for an adequate reply. Open questions facilitate the in-depth expression of opinions, **attitudes**, thoughts and feelings and, as such, are important for the **public relations** practitioner to elicit necessary responses. They also offer the respondent greater control over what is discussed.

See **closed questions, interpersonal communication, questionnaires.**

Open system

A system is an entity made up of components in an interdependent relationship with each other which requires constant adaptation among its parts to maintain organic wholeness and balance. As such, a small group can be seen as an *open* system with relatively permeable boundaries producing a high degree of interchange between the system itself and the environment surrounding it. Within open systems, groups interact freely with their environments as demonstrated in Figure 14. In **closed system**s there exists little interchange between the group and its environment. Its boundaries are more solid and adaptations to the environment are limited.

See **systems theory.**

Galanes, G., Adams, K. and Brilhart, J.(2004) *Effective Group Discussion, Theory and Practice*, 11th edn. New York: McGraw-Hill.

Operating costs

Operating costs centring around both effectiveness and efficiency must be borne in mind when planning a **public relations**

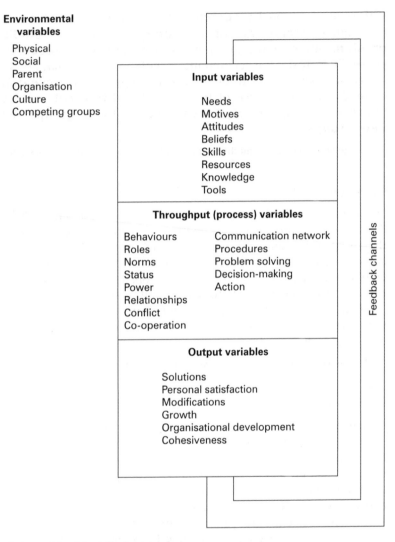

Environmental variables

Physical
Social
Parent
Organisation
Culture
Competing groups

Input variables

Needs
Motives
Attitudes
Beliefs
Skills
Resources
Knowledge
Tools

Throughput (process) variables

Behaviours   Communication network
Roles   Procedures
Norms   Problem solving
Status   Decision-making
Power   Action
Relationships
Conflict
Co-operation

Output variables

Solutions
Personal satisfaction
Modifications
Growth
Organisational development
Cohesiveness

Feedback channels

Figure 14   Model of a group as an open system

programme/plan. These **issue**s will differ depending on the importance of the **message** and the **audience** group or **publics** which the **public relations** practitioner is addressing. In order to be cost-effective, lateral thinking is often necessary to keep costs down. Examples of this might include piggyback mailings (when small inserts are added to established mailings by other organisations at a reduced cost) or joint ventures with complementary organisations or products. Operating costs need to be accounted for when considering the **resources** element of the planning process.

See **public relations programme/plan.**

Opinion formers and leaders

Opinion formers and leaders may be made up of knowledgeable, ignorant or even hostile individuals, but they are trusted because of their apparent or actual authority. They are the **intervening publics** in that they carry a **message** to the **primary publics**. They may be grouped into the following:

- teachers, parents, doctors, academics, clergy;
- community group leaders, politicians, group leaders, trade union officials;
- local government officers and civil servants, officials of quangos;
- presenters, commentators;
- **journalist**s and authors, TV and radio personalities;
- authorities on certain subjects who may write and broadcast;
- officials of institutions, societies, trade associations and professional bodies.

Many of these people hold influence and are therefore important in the **public relations programme/plan**. They often need to be dealt with on an interpersonal and face-to-face basis. There is currently much debate about who the opinion formers and leaders are and where their ideas and opinions come from.

See **flow of influence concept.**

Opinion polls

O

Opinion polls are a form of **marketing research** used to measure the state of opinion, awareness or **attitudes** among certain **publics**. In an opinion poll a sample of **publics** (either a **quota sample** where specific people are chosen according to certain variables, or a **random sample** where names and addresses are picked from a list at regular intervals) are asked simple questions which call for 'yes', 'no' or 'don't know' answers. The results are represented in a graph and subsequent polls, known as tracking polls, are then conducted to measure any shift in opinion or **attitudes** etc. The trends are then calculated and presented in a table to record the results of a **public relations programme/plan**.

Opportunities to see (OTS)

OTS is a rating which measures the potential readership or **audience** of a published story. Each appearance of the story is multiplied by the published circulation or readership figure of each journal, or, in the case of broadcasting, by the published **audience** figures.

Organigraphs

Organigraphs were established to overcome the deficiencies of the straight **organisational chart** which failed to tell employees which parts connected to which and how people and processes should co-ordinate. There are various kinds of organigraph (see Figure 15):

- *Set*: managers allocate tasks.
- *Chain*: managers control.
- *Hub*: managers co-ordinate.
- *Web*: managers link, motivate and energise.

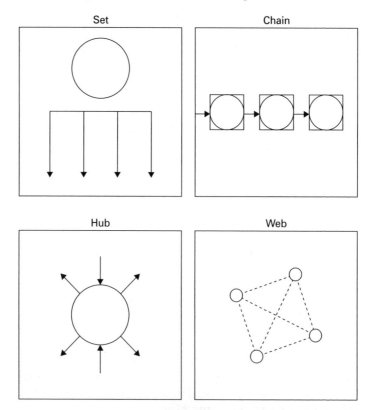

Figure 15   A selection of organigraphs

These are designed better to reflect the way in which people organise themselves at work today. Organigraphs have more to do with relationships and processes than with names, titles and formal authority.

See **organisational chart, organisational structure, organisational structure of public relations.**

Organisational chart

An organisational chart is a pictorial record which shows the formal relations which the organisation intended should prevail within it.

See **hierarchy, organigraphs, organisational structure, organisational structure of public relations, span of control.**

Organisational climate

Organisational climate is sometimes used interchangeably with **organisational culture**, but it has its own precise definition. Climate is a metaphor for understanding the 'atmospherics' and 'temperature' of an organisation. For example, an organisation's climate may be described as calm, turbulent, stormy, heavy, oppressive, cool, thunderous or red-hot. According to organisational theorist Schein (2000, 24), climate is 'embedded in the physical look of the place, the emotionality exhibited by the employees, the experiences of visitors or new employees upon entry and myriad other artefacts that are seen, heard, felt . . . I define climate as a cultural artefact resulting from espoused values and shared tacit assumptions.'

Schein, E. (2000) 'Sense and nonsense about culture and climate', in N. Ashkanasy, C. Wilderom, and M. Peterson (eds) *Handbook of Organizational Culture and Climate*. London: Sage, 22–30.

O

Organisational communication

Organisational communication is the academic field which attempts to understand the way in which participants within an organisation understand and experience organisations. It is important in **public relations** work because employees are considered ambassadors for their organisation and in turn play a diplomatic role. Scholars and practitioners of organisational communication seek to understand:

* patterns and divergences in **attitudes**, perceptions and **values**;
* how to make sense of symbols and language;
* how to manage change;

- how to improve **organisational climate**s for the benefit of service and innovation;
- how to influence career development and manage mergers and acquisitions.

Buchanan, D. and Huczynski, A. (2004) *Organisational Behaviour: An Introductory Text*, 5th edn. Upper Saddle River, NJ: Prentice Hall.

Organisational culture

An organisation's culture focuses on the **values, beliefs, attitudes**, behaviours and meanings used by its members to validate and construct the 'uniqueness' of the nature of the organisation. Sometimes referred to 'as the way we do things around here' (Deal and Kennedy, 1982), it is also referred to as 'the collective programming of the mind' (Hofstede, 2001). Simply put, organisational culture is the collection of relatively uniform and enduring **values, beliefs**, customs, traditions and practices which are shared by an organisation's members, learned by new employees and transmitted from one generation of employees to the next. Increased **globalisation** has placed organisational culture firmly on the agenda, as has the fact that organisational performance depends on employee **values** being aligned with company **strategy**. The use of the term 'culture' in an organisational context has two main readings: the instrumental, in which culture is a method of management control, and the interpretive, in which culture is the lived experience of the organisation as expressed through its members **beliefs, values** and behaviours.

Edgar Schein's (2005) model of culture considers organisational culture in terms of the assumptions which lie behind the **values** which determine the behaviour patterns and the visible artefacts of the organisation, such as architecture, office layout, dress codes, etc. His fundamental view is that culture is the sharing of meanings and the sharing of basic assumptions among employees. He calls the first level of the model 'the manifestation of culture'. It refers to the visible things which the culture produces, such as artefacts, ceremonials, courses, gestures, heroes, jokes, language, legends, mottoes, norms, the physical layout, rites and rituals, sagas, **slogans**, stories and symbols. The second level of the model Schein terms 'organisational values'. These **values** and **beliefs** are often unspoken but mould employees' behaviours. They relate to those things which have personal or organisational worth or meaning to the senior management and are typically based on moral, societal or religious precepts which are learned in childhood and modified through experience. The third level of the model he terms 'basic assumptions'. These are invisible, preconscious and taken-for-granted understandings held by individuals with respect to aspects of human behaviour and the organisation's relationship to its environment. As such, they are difficult to access.

Deal, T. E. and Kennedy, A. A. (1982) *Corporate Cultures: The Rites and Rituals of Corporate Life*. Reading, MA: Addison-Wesley.

Hofstede, G. (2001) *Culture's Consequences: International Differences in Work-Related Values*, 2nd edn. Sage: London.

Schein, E. (2005) *Organisational Culture and Leadership*, 3rd edn. San Francisco: Jossey-Bass Business Books.

Organisational structure

Organisational structure is the formal system of task and reporting relationships which controls, co-ordinates and motivates employees so that they work together to achieve organisational goals. The purpose of organisational structure is first to divide up the organisational activities and allocate them to sub-units and then to control these activities so that all employees work together to achieve the aims and mission of the organisation. Figure 16 illustrates a typical organisational structure.

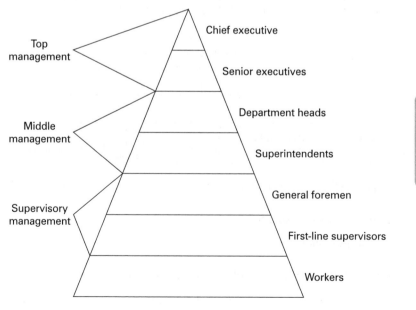

Figure 16   Typical organisational structure

See **hierarchy, organisational chart, organisational structure of public relations, span of control.**

Organisational structure of public relations

The **public relations** operation is normally organised along either task-oriented or functional lines. Smaller, single operations usually have no choice but to do everything under one banner. Organisations which have a **task-oriented structure** where individual tasks are split and delegated to small groups or individuals may look like the model shown in Figure 17.

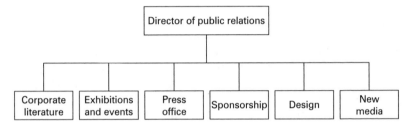

Figure 17   Task-oriented structure

Other organisations may be organised along functional lines, where activities are split and groups or individuals do all the tasks and may look like the model shown in Figure 18.

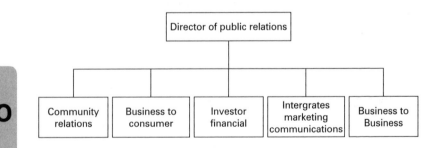

Figure 18   Functional structure

Organisational symbolism

See **visual identity.**

Osgood-Schramm model of communication

Osgood and Schramm created a circular model of communication in 1954 which showed that the receiver as well as the sender

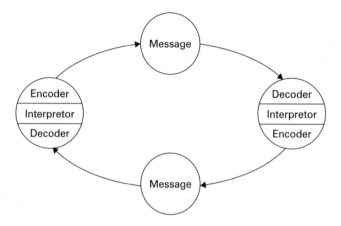

Figure 19   The Osgood-Schramm model of communication

is engaged in a continuous and active act of communication. Each party needs to interpret the sent message and form a response before sending it out or back. The model shown in Figure 19 suggests that communication is endless and flowing. However, one of the limitations of this model is that it does not include a **mass media** role and is far more suited to small group or one-to-one communications. **Feedback** in **mass media** communications is hard to measure but the **Westley-McLean model of communication** attempts to address the role of the **mass media** in communication.

Outputs and outcomes

See **evaluation.**

O

Paradigm

A paradigm is a world-view which frames and influences our approach to everything we see. It is a tool which allows us to make sense of the world around us and consists of the **values** and assumptions we take for granted. In an academic context, including **public relations**, a paradigm will be apparent by references to a concept which does not need to be explained in detail each time it is mentioned.

> *See* **dominant paradigm.**

People power

'People power' is the term used to describe the extent to which ordinary people have the power, through demonstrations, boycotts or litigation, to change the way in which organisations think and act.

> *See* **activism, pressure groups.**

Persuasion

Benoit and Benoit (2008) define persuasion as a process (see Figure 20) in which a source uses a **message** to achieve a goal by creating, changing or reinforcing the **attitudes** of others. Persuasion has four important components:

1. It is goal-directed in that it is a means to an end.
2. It is a process in that persuasion starts with the source or persuader who has a goal. The source then creates a message

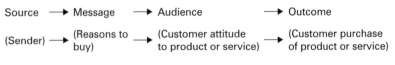

Figure 20   The process of persuasion

which it is hoped will encourage the **audience** to accomplish the source's goal. The message must then be delivered and, if effective, will result in the **audience** complying with the source's wishes.

3 It involves people.

4 It can change, create or reinforce **attitudes**.

Public relations developed as a persuasive communication function. It is planned persuasion to change adverse **public opinion** or to reinforce **public opinion** and the **evaluation** of results for future use. Persuasion relies on 'appeal' rather than 'strength'. There are six types of persuasion:

1 *Reciprocation:* people tend to return a favour, hence the appeal of free samples in **marketing** and **public relations**.

2 *Commitment and consistency:* once people commit either verbally or in writing, they tend to honour that commitment, even if the price of a product or service is raised at the last moment (see **cognitive dissonance**).

3 *Social Proof:* people like to conform and tend to follow the behaviours or purchasing decisions of others.

4 *Authority:* people tend to obey authority figures even if they disagree with the action.

5 *Liking:* people are usually easily persuaded by people they like.

6 *Scarcity:* perceived scarcity can generate demand. Prospects often respond to sales if they are for a 'limited time'.

Table 8   Methods of persuasion

Type of appeal	Route of appeal
By appeal to reason	Logical argument
	Logic
	Rhetoric
	Scientific method
	Proof
By appeal to emotion	**Advertising**
	Faith

P

(Continued)

Table 8   Continued

Type of appeal	Route of appeal
	Public relations
	Presentation and imagination
	Propaganda
	Seduction
	Tradition
	Pity
Aids to persuasion	**Non-verbal communication**
	Communication skills
	Sales **techniques**

Benoit, W. L. and Benoit, P. (2008) *Persuasive Messages: The Process of Influence*. Oxford: Blackwell.

Camp, L. (2007) *Can I Change Your Mind? The Craft and Art of Persuasive Writing*. London, A&C Black.

Cialdini, R. (2007) *Influence: The Psychology of Persuasion*. New York: HarperCollins.

PEST analysis

A PEST analysis forms the first stage of the planning cycle of the **public relations programme/plan** and describes a framework of macroenvironmental factors used in **environmental monitoring** and **boundary spanning**. It is a valuable **technique** used for analysing the external environment of an organisation and the long-term drivers of change. PEST is an acronym for the four main areas which can affect an organisation:

1 Political
2 Economic
3 Social
4 Technological.

Suggested headings for a PEST analysis are outlined in Table 9.

As modern organisations exist in complex environments, a broader grid has been developed – the **EPISTLE**. Added to the

Table 9 Suggested headings for a PEST analysis

Political	Economic
Employment legislation	Economic growth
Environmental legislation	Rise or decrease in interest rates
Trade legislation	Rise or decrease of inflation rate
Change of government	Abundance or lack of money supply and credit
Tax laws	
Tariffs and political stability	Exchange rates
	Levels of (un)employment
	Levels of disposable income
	Business/economic cycles
	Energy costs
Social	**Technological**
Population shifts/growth including immigration/migration	New technological discoveries and incentives
Values and lifestyles	Speed of change
Health-consciousness	Investment in technologies
Age distribution	Spending on **research** and development
Levels of education	Obsolescence
Career **attitudes**	Impact of automation and new technologies
Income and wealth distribution	
Purchasing trends	
Social **attitudes** and concerns	

P

four elements of the PEST analysis are Information, the Legal aspects and the physical Environment.

Armstrong, M. (2006) *A Handbook of Human Resource Management Practice*, 10th edn. London: Kogan Page.

Photo opportunities

A photo opportunity (photo-op) is an opportunity to take a memorable and effective photograph, usually of a celebrity or a politician, in order to generate good **publicity**. The term has recently acquired a negative connotation, referring to carefully planned pseudo-events, sometimes masquerading as news.

Pitch

The **public relations** pitch competitively presents the **public relations programme/plan** to the potential client. Pitching can be known as procurement or **tendering**.

Podcast

A podcast is a collection of digital media files which is distributed over the internet for playback on personal computers or portable media players. Podcasts can be listened to on an MP3 player, on a computer using media player software or by calling a virtual phone number. Podcasts allow people to share information and, as such, are a useful **public relations tool**. Podcasting gives **public relations** practitioners another way to connect with the client's existing and prospective target **audience**. If the contents of the podcast are newsworthy, it brings extra opportunities to promote an organisation. Information from the organisation will be sent automatically to subscribers who have expressed an interest in its products, services or areas of expertise.

www.forimmediaterelease.biz
www.forward-moving.com/blog/category/podcast

Point of sale

The point of sale is the immediate area surrounding the cash till. It is hoped that queuing customers will make impulse buys from the point of sale.

Austin, T. E. (2000) *New Retail Power and Muscle: Remarkable Weapon to Win the War at the Point of Sale*, BRG Publishing.

Political communication

Political communication is carried out by political parties both internally and externally. Political communication consists of **media relations**, personal **public relations, reputation management, image and impression management, speech-writing/ speech-making** and political **marketing**. Political **marketing** consists of **segmentation, demographics** and **market research**.

McNair, B. (2007) *An Introduction to Political Communication*. London: Routledge.

Moloney, K. (2006) *Rethinking Public Relations? The Spin and the Substance* (2nd edn). London: Routledge.

PR Week

PR Week is the weekly **trade journal** of news, **analysis** and jobs for **public relations** practitioners and is published by Haymarket.

www.prweek.com

Press agentry

See **Grunig's four models of public relations.**

Press Association

The Press Association is the national news agency of the UK and Ireland, covering all important news 24 hours a day, 365 days a year. From the core newswire services to video bulletins for digital platforms, the Press Association provides a continuous stream of news, images, information and data. It has a network of news and sports reporters, photographers and video **journalist**s around the country and key locations overseas covering all major breaking stories.

See **external media support.**

www.pressassociation.co.uk

P

Press clippings

Clippings are taken of press **articles** and **features** as part of the **evaluation** process of the **public relations programme/plan**. The contents of these clippings are measured and reviewed to identify if the intended **messages** were communicated accurately and with understanding.

Press Complaints Commission (PCC)

The PCC is an independent body which deals with complaints from members of the public about the **editorial** content of newspapers and magazines. It is a free service to complainants.

www.pcc.org.uk

Press conference

See **news conference, press reception.**

Press officer

A press officer is the individual who practises **media relations** on behalf of the organisation or client and, as such, needs to be pro-active as well as reactive. Sometimes known as the **media relations** officer, the press officer has two primary responsibilities:

1 to initiate media coverage;
2 to supply information on demand by the media.

The advantages of the role of press officer are that:

- the press officer has access to information needed by **journalist**s;
- the press officer has time to check the facts before submitting information to **journalist**s;
- any press officer who is a member of the **Chartered Institute of Public Relations (CIPR)** has a duty of accuracy under the **Code of Professional Conduct**;
- the press officer can counsel organisational leaders to give a media interview when they may be reluctant to do so.

The disadvantages are that:

- the press officer may be coerced by the organisation to present stories to the media which have little news value;
- the press officer may be perceived as lacking status and authority;
- the press officer may be viewed by the media as biased and therefore untrustworthy;
- the press officer may be caught between the organisational management and the media, especially in a **crisis** situation.

Baines, P., Egan, J. and Jefkins, F. (2004) *Public Relations, Contemporary Issues and Techniques*. Oxford: Elsevier Butterworth-Heinemann, Chapter 3 – The Role of the Press Officer.

P

Press packs

A press pack (sometimes called a media pack) is a pack of background information and key facts on a company, organisation, event, service or product which is distributed to **journalist**s. The press pack can act as an introduction to the organisation, informing **journalist**s who the organisation is and what it does, or it can provide information on a specific event, service or product. Press packs make the lives of **journalist**s easier by providing all the information they need and they increase the possibility of media coverage. Press packs usually include some or all of the following:

- background information on the organisation, service or product
- **website** details for the organisation
- the purpose/**mission statement**
- relevant position statements
- interesting facts and figures
- financial information
- key dates and events
- the organisational structure
- biographical information about key people
- photographs
- product samples.

See **news conference, press reception.**

Press reception

A press reception is a more planned and hospitable event than a **press conference**. A press reception has a newsworthy story, product or event to communicate to the media and is often planned and targeted months in advance. Refreshments, **timetables**, presentations, product demonstrations and **press packs** should be available at press receptions.

See **events management, news conference.**

P

Press release

The press release (also known as the **news release**) is one of the most important communication **tools** of the **public relations** practitioner and is used extensively in the field of **media relations**. It is an announcement of news sent to the media on behalf of the organisation. Press releases are written in a predetermined, formulaic way. The press release is one of the most effective forms of **publicity**. **Editorial** coverage produces more enquiries than paid – for advertisements, usually because readers read a publication for its news rather than for its adverts. Successful releases have two merits:

1 they are written in a **journalist**ic format;
2 they are newsworthy.

Every newsworthy story has three vital parts:

1 the **headline**
2 the first sentence
3 subsequent paragraphs and body copy.

The headline should sum up the story in ten words or less. It should not be too clever or too obscure but should be simple and comprehensible. The first sentence should sum up all the main points of story. It should tell the reader who has done what, where, why, when and how. This is known as the 5 Ws and H:

- *Who* is the story about?
- *What* happened or is going to happen?
- *When* did it happen or is it going to happen?
- *Where* did it happen or is it going to happen?
- *Why* did it happen or is it going to happen?
- *How* did it come about or is it going to come about?

The **SOLAADS** seven-point model expands on the 5Ws and H:

- *Subject*: what is the story about?
- *Organisation*: what is the name of the organisation?
- *Location*: what is the location of the organisation?
- *Advantages*: what is new, special or beneficial about the product or service?
- *Applications*: how and by whom can the product or service be enjoyed?
- *Details*: what are the specifications and details with regard to the colour, size, price, etc.?
- *Source*: what is the source if this is different from the location?

The press release should be to the point and should not contain any non-essential information. The subsequent paragraphs should add extra information in order of importance. Editors delete paragraphs from the end of the release, so vital news should not be left to the end. Press releases should be factual and state the **benefits** of the product or service communicated. Quotes allow for **observations** and points of view. They also allow the writer of the release to make a claim that need not be substantiated and they are free from the rigorous analysis of the ordinary text.

P

The best topics for a press release are often:

- new products
- an unusual product or company
- a new factory or investment
- a new division or restructuring
- record sales, exports or financial results
- new appointments or **promotion**s
- charity events, community activities, **sponsorship**s or awards
- the case study (see **case studies**) or application story
- celebrity visits or **endorsement**s
- Survey and report findings

Bartram (2006) suggests a 14-step approach to writing the press release:

1 Know the point of the story.
2 Check the story passes the 'so what?' test. This checks the story's newsworthiness and therefore the likelihood of it being accepted by a **journalist**.
3 Assemble all the needed information.
4 Judge the weight of the story. Decide how important the story is likely to be for the **journalist**s who receive it.
5 Focus on the target **audience**.
6 Write the introduction.
7 Write the remaining copy.
8 Add a note to editors with further information (if needed).
9 Write the headline.
10 Add date and contact details.
11 Add a note about other **resources** and details about how to obtain them.
12 Edit the release.
13 Get the press release approved for distribution.
14 Conduct a final check.

Bartram, P. (2006) *How to Write the Perfect Press Release*. Brighton: New Venture Publishing.

Pressure groups

Pressure groups are groups of people who join together in order to put 'pressure' on the Government to force through legislative or political changes. They can be divided into two categories:

1 *cause groups* who lobby for policy **objectives** such as electoral reform or animal rights;

2 *sectional groups* who represent a section of society, such as teachers or farmers.

They are an important group of **publics** for **public relations** practitioners to communicate with as they hold the power to force an organisation into a **crisis** situation.

See **active publics, activism.**

Primary publics

Primary publics are those **publics** who can or cannot do what the organisation wants or needs to be done.

See **publics.**

Primary research

Primary research is sometimes referred to as field **research** and is the collecting of original data. There are various methods of collecting primary research, including **observation**, experiments, **surveys** and consumer panels.

See **qualitative research methods, quantitative research methods, research.**

Probing questions

Probing or *secondary* questions are used by the questioner as a method of eliciting further and more-in-depth information following the initial question and response. The ability to probe effectively is therefore at the core of effective questioning and is a vital means of information-gathering for the **public relations** practitioner.

See **closed questions, interpersonal communication, open questions, questionnaires.**

Hargie, O. (2006) *The Handbook of Communication Skills*, 3rd edn. London: Routledge.

P

Problem recognition

People do not usually think about a situation unless they believe that something needs to be done to 'fix' it, i.e. unless they have an actual or a potential problem. A group of people who are thinking about a problem and are actively seeking information about that problem soon fall into the **paradigm** of **active** or **aware publics**. These are the people with whom **public relations** practitioners must seek to communicate and whom they persuade through a **two-way symmetrical** dialogue.

See **publics.**

Problem-solving process facilitator

The problem-solving process facilitator is one of the three main types of managerial role falling within the main role of the **communication manager.** The facilitator helps others in the organisation to solve their **public relations** problems, and counsels or advises on the **public relations programme/plan**. The problem-solving facilitator is a role often filled by specialist **consultancies**.

Product recall

Products are recalled when they are found to be defective or faulty. It is the responsibility of the **public relations** practitioner to recall these products speedily and effectively so that the defect can be remedied. The key to product recall is speed but the urgency of advertisements should be tempered with reassurance. There is some **research** (Bejou and Palmer, 1998) which suggests that a satisfactory response to a problem may lead to greater levels of satisfaction than existed prior to the problem. Effective **public relations** means admitting immediately that the product is faulty and organising the speediest possible recall so that the defect can be remedied before further damage is done.

Bejou, D. and Palmer, A. (1998) 'Service failure and loyalty: An exploratory empirical study of airline customers', *Journal of Services Marketing*, 12 ,1, 7–22.

Product/service life cycle (activities of public relations)

Different kinds of **public relations** activity is required at each of the six different stages of a product or service life cycle (see Figure 21):

1 *Development:* at this stage **public relations** practitioners work closely with **research** and development personnel. Media awareness of the product or service is developed. The focus is on **stakeholder** compliance.
2 *Introduction:* at this stage **public relations** will usually involve **press release**s and **news conferences** and **product launches** for suppliers in order to promote awareness of the product or service.

P

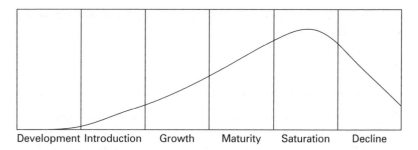

Development Introduction   Growth   Maturity   Saturation   Decline

Figure 21   The traditional product life cycle

3 *Growth:* this is a stage of competition and **public relations** practitioners will need to focus on **internal relations.** If the organisation is seeking funds, the **public relations** practitioner will also need to ensure that business prospects are reported favourably in the financial press.

4 *Maturity:* **public relations** functions at this stage to maintain sales and to identify future **marketing** opportunities and product and/or service development.

5 *Saturation:* when demand for the product or service drops, **public relations** has a role to play in mergers and acquisitions. The **public relations** practitioner may also have to deal with the media if there are any **industrial relations** problems. Alternatively, if a new product or service has been identified, **public relations** will be needed to create awareness.

6 *Eventual decline:* the function of **public relations** at this stage is to end the life of the product or service in a dignified manner while keeping all **stakeholders** informed.

Professional bodies in the UK

Chartered Institute of Public Relations (CIPR) (www.ipr.org.uk)
Public Relations Consultants Association (PRCA) (www.prca. org.uk)
International Public Relations Association (IPRA) (www.ipra.org)
Global Alliance for Public Relations and Communication Management (www.globalpr.org/new)

Professionalism and regulation

There currently exists a debate about whether the discipline of **public relations** is a profession or not, especially as it has its roots in **press**

agentry and **propaganda.** The *Concise Oxford Dictionary* defines a profession as 'a vocation or calling, especially one that involves some branch of advanced learning or science'. Elton (1993, 137) suggests the following prerequisites for a profession and from these it is clear that **public relations** *can* be considered a profession:

- an underlying discipline or cognitive base;
- a body of practitioners;
- a disciplinary organisation;
- induction, training and licensing of members;
- communication channels between members;
- self-reflection, leading to improvement;
- corporate **evaluation** and **feedback**;
- a code of **ethics** and accountability to the profession;
- corporate accountability to society;
- quality assurance of the profession;
- the ability to ensure high standards of remuneration.

Cutlip *et al.* (1985, 72) add the following conditions:

- specialised educational preparation to acquire knowledge and skills based on a body of theory developed through **research**;
- provision of a unique and essential service which is recognised as such by the community;
- an emphasis on public service and responsibility;
- the autonomy and personal responsibility of members;
- a self-governing association of colleagues to enforce codes of **ethics** and standards of performance.

The establishment of professional bodies such as the **Chartered Institute of Public Relations (CIPR)** in the UK and the **Public Relations Society of America (PRSA)** in the United States have led to the introduction of **Codes of Professional Conduct** and calls for regulation of particular sections of the industry, such as **lobbying.**

Cutlip, S. M., Center, A. H. and Broom, G. M. (1985) *Effective Public Relations*, 6th edn. Englewood Cliffs, NJ: Prentice Hall.
Elton, L. (1993) 'University teaching: A professional model for quality', in R. Ellis (ed.) *Quality Assurance for University Teaching*. Milton Keynes: Open University Press.

Promotion

Promotion involves communicating information about a product, **brand** or company. It makes up one of the four key elements of the

marketing mix, the other three being product management, pricing and distribution. Promotion is generally divided into two parts:

1 ***Above-the-line*** *promotion:* promotion in the media for which the advertiser pays a fee, e.g. television, radio, newspapers, the internet.
2 ***Below-the-line*** *promotion:* all other types of promotion, some of which can be subtle, e.g. **sponsorship**, **product placement**, **endorsement**s, **sales promotion**, **merchandising**, **direct mail,** personal selling, **public relations**, trade shows and **exhibitions.**

> Clow, K. E. (2007) *Integrated Advertising, Promotion and Marketing Communications*, 3rd edn. Upper Saddle Row, NJ: Prentice Hall.

Proofs

First proofs are copies of a manuscript (or any other written communication) sent by the publisher or printer for **copy-editing**. Final proofs show the page layout, the position of any illustrations, the index and details such as the cover design.

Propaganda

Propaganda impartially presents information to a mass **audience** in order to influence and persuade their decisions, **beliefs** and actions. Propaganda works best when it presents the truth, but it is more likely to present facts selectively or to give a loaded **message** to induce an emotional rather than a rational response. Propaganda was originally a neutral term used to describe the communicating of information, but during the twentieth century the term acquired the negative connotation of the dissemination of false claims to support political ideologies. The propagandist seeks to change the way in which people think about an **issue** by preventing them from having access to an opposing point of view. Propaganda may be divided into different categories:

* *White propaganda* comes from an identified source and is characterised by **public relations** and the one-sided presentation of an argument (see **Grunig's four models of public relations**).
* *Black propaganda,* such as disinformation, is untrue. It is identified as being from one source but is in fact from another. It is often used to disguise the fact that the information may originally have generated from an organisation with a negative **image**.

- *Grey propaganda* is propaganda without any identifiable source or author.

Below are a selection of **techniques** used for generating propaganda:

- *Ad hominem*: a Latin term for attacking one's opponents rather than their argument.
- *Appeal to authority*: this cites prominent people who support the action or argument.
- *Appeal to fear*: this seeks to build support by installing fears or anxieties in the population.
- *Appeal to prejudice*: this uses emotive terms to fix value or moral goodness to an idea or course of action.
- *Argumentum ad nauseam*: this is the constant repetition of an idea which is eventually taken as the truth.
- *Bandwagon*: this encourages people to take the same course of action that everyone else is taking.
- *Black and white fallacy*: this presents only two choices (either/or).
- *Beautiful people*: this is regularly used in **advertising**. The advertisement shows attractive, happy people and the prospects believe that if they buy the product they too will be attractive and happy.
- *Big Lie*: this is the repeated telling of a complex set of events used to justify subsequent action.
- *Common man*: the propagandist presents his ideas as those of the 'common man'. This is designed to win confidence.
- *Demonizing the enemy*: this makes those who have a different viewpoint appear to be subhuman.
- *Disinformation*: this is the creation or deletion of information from public records.
- *Glittering generalities*: these are emotionally appealing words applied to a product or an idea.
- ***Slogans***: these are brief and strident statements which may include labelling or stereotyping.
- *Quotes out of context*: this is the selective editing of quotes which can change meanings.
- ***Testimonials***: these are quotations used in or out of context to support a product or idea.

Maloney, K. (2006) *Rethinking Public Relations, PR, Propaganda and Democracy*, 2nd edn. Abingdon: Routledge.

O'Shaughnessy. N. (2004) *Politics and Propaganda, Weapons of Mass Seduction*. Manchester: Manchester University Press.

P

Properties and product placement

Many products are used on film and television sets. The supply of these products is termed 'product placement'. Another term is 'presence **advertising**' which means making payments for using products as props (or properties).

See **sponsorship.**

Proposals

A report or proposition spells out what **public relations** actions the practitioner or consultant recommends. Propositions are based on thorough **research** and should be set out clearly in an objective and factual style. The information should be set out in a logical and comprehensible sequence. The proposal should be preceded by a brief (a statement of the purpose, scope and limitations of the proposal) and a summary which offers a concise and actionable overview of the proposals. All pages should be numbered and a contents list or index is vital. Table 10 offers a draft layout for a **public relations** consultancy proposal.

See **report-writing.**

Table 10 Public relations consultancy proposal

Section	Content
Title Page	This section should state for whom and by whom the proposal has been prepared.
Contents	This section should give chapter or section headings with page numbers.
Summary	This section should include the findings or proposals.
The brief	This section should be as instructed by the client.
Experience statement	This section should set out the consultant's experience with similar clients.
Personnel	This section should offer background details on individuals involved in the project.
Situation	**PEST analysis** and **SWOT analysis**, as **research**ed by the consultant.

(Continued)

Table 10   Continued

Section	Content
Recommendations	This section should outline the consultant's plan of action.
Budget	This section should detail costs, methods and timing of payments.
Brag list	This section should list past and present clients.
Appendices	This section should offer relevant appendices, if applicable.

Psychographics

In the field of **marketing**, **public relations**, opinion **research** and social **research** in general, psychographic variables are any attributes relating to personality, **values**, **attitudes**, interests and lifestyles. They differ from demographic variables (such as age and gender) and behavioural variables (such as loyalty).

See **demographics.**

Psyops

Psyops stands for psychological operations or 'political warfare'. Psyops draws on persuasive communication and its purpose is to affect the perceptions, **attitudes** and opinions of others in order to influence their behaviour. Although psyops takes its influence from military **propaganda**, its methods of persuasive communication are linked to the practice of **public relations**. Psyops programmes require information about targets – friendly, neutral and hostile – and should include:

- the identification of key **publics** and **stakeholders** (both friendly and hostile);
- the identification of the **beliefs**, **attitudes** and behaviours of key **publics** and **stakeholders**;
- the **analysis** of the weaknesses of key **publics** and **stakeholders** within the society;
- the determination of the **message** and its most effective method of transmission to reach the desired target;
- the impact of psyops communication.

P

The practice of psyops obviously raises ethical questions for **public relations** practitioners as any form of persuasive communication must question accountability.

See **persuasion, propaganda.**

Public affairs

Public affairs is a specialist area of practice within **public relations** which is concerned with those relationships involved in public policy-making, legislation and regulation which may affect the interests of organisations and their operations. Public affairs consultants use their understanding of the political system to offer political and public policy advice to their clients who may include private sector companies, not-for-profit organisations or overseas governments. Public affairs consultants also identify key **stakeholders** in the decision- making process in European, national, regional and local government bodies. They work to maintain relationships with these individuals and to assist clients to promote and protect their interests effectively.

See **lobbying.**

White, J. (1991) *How To Understand and Manage Public Relations*. London: Business Books.

Public information campaign

A **public relations programme/plan** or campaign delivered to the public which uses the one-way **public information model**. This is most usually used by local government to spread **messages** to constituents and local residents.

See **Grunig's four models of public relations, publics.**

Public information model

See **Grunig's four models of public relations.**

Public media

Public media represent all channels owned and operated by third-party media organisations (as opposed to public broadcasting) and are in the business of creating **audience**s primarily for

P

the advertisers who fund them. Public media can be employed in **public relations** in a number of ways:

- *Publicity*: involves obtaining **editorial** coverage in the news and information sections of **mass media**. Public media are reliant on **public relations** for providing this information at little or no cost.
- *Entertainment programming*: heightens public consciousness of a wide range of ideologies, **issue**s and products.
- *Paid-for **image** and event **advertising***: used more and more by profit and **non-profit** organisations alike.

The key challenge in using public media is to capture the attention of **audience**s in a highly competitive environment. Any **public relations** story must be attractive and newsworthy to potential media producers.

Public opinion

Public opinion is generally considered to be a difficult term to define. Edward **Bernays** called it 'a term describing an ill-defined, mercurial and changeable group of individual judgements'. The best way to understand the concept is to split the two components: 'public' and 'opinion'. Public signifies a group of people who hold things in common, while an opinion is the expression of an **attitude** on a particular **issue.** When **attitudes** become strong enough, they manifest as opinions. When opinions become strong enough, they manifest as verbal or behavioural actions. Public opinion therefore represents a consensus. Trying to influence an individual's **attitude** is the main focus of a **public relations** practitioner's role.

Bernays, E. (1923) *Crystallising Public Opinion*. New York: Liveright.

Public relations (PR)

According to the **Chartered Institute of Public Relations (CIPR),** 'Public relations is the planned and sustained effort to establish and maintain goodwill and **mutual understanding** between an organisation and its publics . . . Public relations is about reputation – the result of what you do, what you say and what others say about you' and 'Public relations practice is the discipline which looks after reputation with the aim of earning understanding and support and influencing opinion and behaviour.'

In practice, **public relations** is a management function which covers a broad range of activities and purposes. However, it should

P

always be regarded as two-way and interactive, deliberate, intentional, planned and in the public interest. **Public relations** can be:

- *representational*: relies on **rhetoric**, oratory and/or advocacy;
- *dialogic*: based on **negotiation, persuasion** and bridge-building;
- *advisory*: fulfils the **counselling role**.

Baines, P., Egan, J. and Jefkins, F. (2004) *Public Relations, Contemporary Issues and Techniques*. Oxford: Elsevier Butterworth-Heinemann.

www.cipr.co.uk

Public Relations Consultants Association (PRCA)

The PRCA is the voice of **public relations consultancies** in the UK. The trade association was set up in 1969 and is based at over 160 offices throughout the UK. The PRCA exists to help members be a better business and demonstrate the value of **public relations** consultancy.

www.prca.org.uk

Public relations programme/plan

A public relations programme/plan (sometimes referred to as a campaign) is a tactical document based on in-depth **research** which outlines the **strategy** of the **public relations** initiatives. According to Anne **Gregory** (2004), planning is vital because it:

- focuses effort;
- improves effectiveness;
- encourages the long-term view;
- helps demonstrate value for money;
- minimises mishaps;
- reconciles conflicts;
- facilitates proactivity.

The plan should answer the questions shown in Table 11.

There are four basic steps to the strategic planning model, as shown in Figure 22.

The ten stages of planning are:

- **analysis**
- **objectives**
- **publics**
- **messages**

P

Table 11   Public relations plan

Key questions	Key variables
What should the plan achieve?	What are the plan's **objectives**?
Who should the plan talk to?	Who are the organisation's publics?
What does the plan want to say?	What are the **messages** the plan should get across?
How shall the plan say it?	Which mechanisms should the plan use to relay the required **messages**?
Has the plan worked?	How should the plan be evaluated?

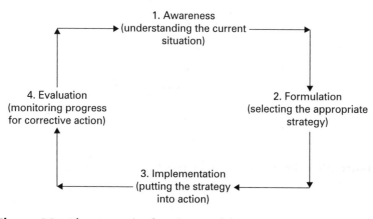

Figure 22   The strategic planning model

- **strategy**
- **tactics**
- **timescales**
- **resources**
- **evaluation**
- **review**.

Figure 23 sets out these stages in a logical order.

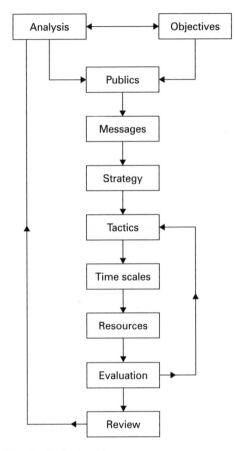

Figure 23 The logical planning process

P

The following list offers a little more detail and explanation of the linear planning process.

- **environmental scanning** and **research** (including **issues analysis**);
- **situation analysis** (historical review plus developing scenarios);
- organisational and market strengths, weaknesses, opportunities and threats (**SWOT analysis**);
- benchmarking against competitor organisations;
- combining internal and external intelligence;

- identifying key **publics**, **research**ing, understanding and classifying in relation to organisation and current **issue**s;
- aiming and supporting **research**able **objectives**;
- **messages**;
- technique selection in the light of **budget** and time constraints;
- communication;
- **evaluation**, review and **analysis** involving key **publics** and **stakeholders** – exploring both positive and negative **feedback**.

See **evaluation, messages, objectives, public relations, resources, strategic planning, tactics, timescales.**

Gregory, A. (2004) *Planning and Managing a Public Relations Campaign.* London: Kogan Page.

Public Relations Society of America (PRSA)

The PRSA is based in New York. It is the world's largest organisation for **public relations** professionals and has almost 32,000 professional and student members.

www.prsa.org

Public speaking

Public speaking is the process of speaking to a group of people in a structured, deliberate manner intended to inform, persuade, influence or entertain. It can be used as a powerful **public relations tool** or **technique.**

Forsyth, P. (2006) *How to Craft Successful Business Presentations and Effective Public Speaking.* London: Foulsham.
Khan-Panni, P. (2007) *Getting Your Point Across.* Oxford: How To Books.

Public sphere

The public sphere is a place where private opinions can be transformed into a more general **public opinion** in relation to democratic procedures and state policy decisions. It is where **issue**s are debated and policy is made. Which views are heard and taken notice of depends on how information is managed in society. Media sociologist Jurgen Habermas (1989) criticised the role of **public relations** in this process, claiming that **public relations** 'engineers consent' by bestowing authority on objects and **issue**s of public interest. Habermas suggested that **public relations** has the ability to set the

P

agenda and thus interrupt the bottom-up flow from citizens to those in power. It is important for **public relations** practitioners to look beyond the **propaganda** model interpretation of the public sphere in which organisations who can afford **public relations** services are able to dominate the news agenda. However, there is no doubt that current media performance has led to **audience** cynicism.

Habermas, J. (1989) *The Structural Transformation of the Public Sphere: An Inquiry into the Category of Bourgeois Society*. Cambridge: Polity.

Publicity

Publicity falls under the **press agentry** model. It is usually generated by publicists and **spin** doctors, often with manipulation of the media involved. Publicity should not be confused with **public relations** in its true sense.

See **Clifford (Max), Grunig's four models of public relations.**

Publicity stunts

Publicity stunts are also referred to as stunts. Publicity stunts are events specially designed to draw the public's attention to the promoters or their causes. They can range from the fun and trivial to the serious and dangerous. A stunt is defined as 'an unusual or difficult feat requiring great skill or daring; especially one performed or undertaken chiefly to gain attention or **publicity**'. The challenge to those who create publicity stunts is to design an event in such a way that the message is integral rather than blurred, that the stunt promotes the concept behind it.

Shankman, P. (2007) *Can We Do That?! Outrageous PR Stunts that Work*. Hoboken, NJ: Wiley.

P

Publics

The 'general' public does not exist as far as the discipline of **public relations** is concerned. Publics are the 'categorised' **audience**s and **stakeholders** who relate to a particular organisation. They are the people, both groups and individuals, with whom a **public relations** practitioner must communicate. As such, they are the consumers of *targeted organisational **messages***.

James **Grunig** describes four types of **publics**:

1 **non-publics**
2 **latent publics**

3 **aware publics**
4 **active publics**.

Active publics can be further broken down into three categories:

1 **all-issue publics**
2 **single-issue publics**
3 **hot-issue publics**.

Publics which are general to most organisations are shown in Figure 24.

See **situational theory of publics, stakeholders, stakeholder model.**

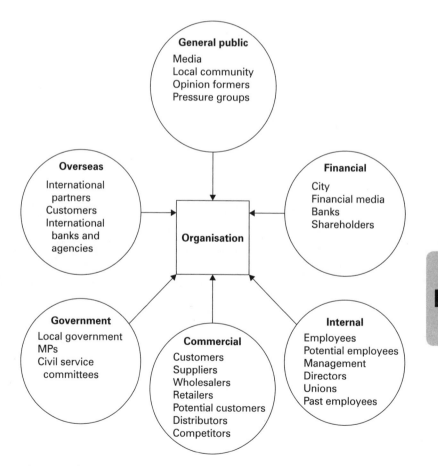

Figure 24   Publics general to most organisations

Puffery

Puffery is a term referring to **promotion**al statements and claims which express laudatory and unfounded, subjective views which are often difficult to take seriously. Puffery is a feature of many **testimonial**s. Puffery often uses the superlative form of a word, for example 'best' and 'the greatest'.

P

Qualitative research methods

Qualitative **research** investigates the reasons for human behaviour. It considers the *why* and *how* of decision-making, as compared to the *what, where* and *when* of **quantitative research**. **Public relations research**ers use qualitative methods to observe a situation or the outcome of a programme. Qualitative **research** in **public relations** generally has four characteristics:

1. *Naturalistic observation:* **research**ers get as close to fully immersing themselves in the situation of the participants as possible.
2. *Contextualisation:* **research**ers look at the total context in which an effect occurs and do not restrict themselves to a few statistical measurements of variables.
3. *Maximised comparisons:* **research**ers do not limit themselves to a few hypotheses which affect only a few people but look at the total public, the total community or the total organisation and make comparisons with similar units.
4. *Sensitised concepts:* **research**ers use language which describes the actual responses of the target groups to a programme in the language they would use to achieve understanding.

Other types of **qualitative research methods** include:

- **focus groups**
- **observation**
- **interviews**
- **content analysis**.

Quantitative research methods

Quantitative **research** measures empirical evidence – information dealing with numbers and anything which can be measured. It generally uses scientific methods which include:

- the generation of models, theories and hypotheses;
- the development of instruments and methods for measurement;

- the manipulation of variables;
- the collection of empirical data;
- the modelling and **analysis** of data;
- the **evaluation** of results.

In **public relations**, quantitative research methods are used for examining, analysing and interpreting **observation**s for the purpose of discovering underlying meanings and patterns of relationships. **Qualitative research methods** might be used to understand the meaning of the numbers produced by quantitative methods. A combination of data-gathering is sometimes referred to as mixed-methods **research**.

Davies, M. Brett (2007) *Doing a Successful Research Project Using Qualitative and Quantitative Methods*. Basingstoke: Palgrave Macmillan.

Questionnaires

Questionnaires are **research tools** used to gather information from a series of questions. Questionnaires can use both **qualitative research methods** and **quantitative research methods** to collect data, according to the type of questions asked. The advantage of using questionnaires is the fact that they are cheap to administer. However, they can have a low response rate. With the increasing use of the internet, on-line questionnaires have become a popular way of collecting information. The main advantages of using on-line questionnaires is that the **research**er has greater flexibility; questions may be displayed using check boxes, pull-down menus, pop-up menus, help screens and **graphics**. An on-line forum also allows responses to be received more quickly from subjects.

Bulmer. M. (ed.) (2004) *Questionnaires*. London: Sage.
Sapsford, R. (2007) *Survey Research*, 2nd edn. London: Sage.

Quota sample

A quota sample is where specific numbers of people of a particular sex, age and social group are found by interviewers. It is the opposite of a **random sample**.

RACE

The RACE model describes a process of **public relations** suggested by Marston (1979). RACE stands for:

- **R**esearch
- **A**ction plan
- **C**ommunication
- **E**valuation.

One criticism of the model is that, because the final step is that of **evaluation**, it takes little account of previously established relationships within **public relations** and implies that friendships resulting from one instance of programming are not relevant or valuable to future efforts.

Marston, J. R. (1979) *Modern Public Relations*. New York: McGraw Hill.

Random sample

A random sample of respondents provides a cross-section of the sample population by selecting names and addresses from a list taken at regular intervals.

See **quota sample.**

Readability formulas

Readability formulas are used as a method of measuring whether members of the public or organisational subsystems have retained a **message** by measuring how easy or difficult it is for an individual to read and understand a piece of writing. The easier it is for people to understand a message, the more likely it is that they will retain the message. All of the most widely used readability formulas, including the Flesch Reading Ease formula, the Gunning Fog Index and the Farr-Jenkins-Patterson formula, have two components: the level of difficulty of the words and the length of the sentences. They use the number of syllables in a word as a measure of word difficulty.

Weiss, C. H. (1972) *Evaluation Research: Methods for Assessing Program Effectiveness*. Englewood Cliffs, NJ: Prentice Hall.

Relationship between marketing and public relations

The relationship between marketing and public relations has always been ambiguous and is often referred to as a 'turf war', both sides wanting to claim the **benefits** for their own discipline. Kotler and Mindak (1978) identified five models of the relationship between marketing and public relations:

1 *Separate but equal functions* – this is the traditional view where **marketing** exists to identify and meet customer needs at a profit. **Public relations** serves to create and maintain goodwill towards a company from its various **publics**, in order for it to be able to achieve its goals (see Figure 25).

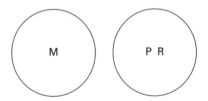

Figure 25   Marketing and public relations – separate but equal functions

2 *Equal but overlapping functions* – **marketing** and **public relations** share some common ground, such as product **publicity** and customer relations. **Public relations** also serves as a counterbalance to the policies of **marketing** departments, advising marketers on the possible wider social implications and reactions to their policies (see Figure 26).

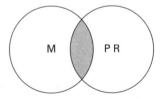

Figure 26   Marketing and public relations – equal but overlapping functions

3 **Marketing** *as the dominant function* – the **public relations** function exists to serve the needs of the **marketing** function. It rejects the idea that **public relations** should exist to help balance the interests of an organisation and of its **publics** and supports the idea that the organisation's needs should come before any social good (see Figure 27).

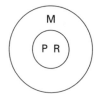

Figure 27   Marketing as the dominant function

4 **Public relations** *as the dominant function* – this is the minority view and argues that the prosperity and ultimate survival of an organisation depends on how it is viewed by its **stakeholders** (see Figure 28).

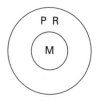

Figure 28   Public relations as the dominant function

5 **Marketing** *and* **public relations** *as convergent functions* – this model holds the view that **marketing** and **public relations** are two functions whose methods and concepts are rapidly converging, leading to **integrated marketing communications (IMC)** (see Figure 29).

R

Figure 29   Marketing and public relations as convergent functions

Public relations can play a corrective role in relation to **marketing**, providing another perspective with regard to management decisions and helping management to balance economic considerations against possible wider social implications. Daniel Edelman, head of one of the world's largest **public relations consultancies**, suggested at the annual conference of the **Public Relations Society of America (PRSA)** in 1989, that **public relations** is most effective when supporting **marketing objectives** in the following scenarios:

- where there is a revolutionary new product – one that can make the news;
- where the company is small and has little money for **advertising**;
- where television advertising is unavailable for regulatory reasons, as in the case of alcohol;
- where there is hostility towards a product or company which needs to be corrected.

He further suggests that **public relations** tends to be more effective than **advertising** when:

- generating new excitement about existing products;
- a company is having difficulties in distributing a product;
- the **advertising** is well-liked but failing to build **brand** recognition;
- a product is relatively complex and takes time to explain;
- regulations make it impossible to advertise a product;
- established products or companies are aligned with a cause.

Kotler, P. and Mindak, W. (1978) 'Marketing and public relations, should they be partners or rivals?', *Journal of Marketing*, 42, 10, 13–20.
Ries, A. and Ries, L. (2004) *The Fall of Advertising and the Rise of PR*. New York: Harper Business.

R

Relationship management

Simply put, relationship management is about building relationships with **publics** who constrain or enhance the ability of an organisation to meet its goal. Relationship management is the term given to the ultimate aim of **public relations**. The purpose and direction of an organisation and its mission is affected by relationships with key constituents in the organisation's environment. The notion of relationship management is based on many factors, including successful **interpersonal communication**, **organisational**

communication and social psychology. Leddingham and Brunning (1998) identified the five major relationship dimensions drawn from **interpersonal communication**s, **marketing** and **public relations** which have most impact on the organisation–consumer relationship. These are trust, openness, involvement, investment of time and effort, and commitment.

Leddingham, J. A. and Brunning, S. D. (1998) Relationship development in public relations: Dimensions of an organization–public relationship, *Public Relations Review*, 24,1, 55–65.

Leadingham, J. A. and Brunning, S. D. (eds) (2000) *Public Relations as Relationship Management: A Relational Approach to the Study and Practice of Public Relations*. Mahwah, NJ: Lawrence Erlbaum.

Relationship marketing

'Relationship marketing' is a term for **public relations**, often put forward by marketers, and sometimes seen as a 'turf-grabbing' exercise by **public relations** practitioners.

See **relationship between marketing and public relations.**

Report-writing

See **proposals.**

Reputation management

The reputation management of an organisation or client is an aim of **public relations**. A good reputation is an organisation's greatest asset and has to be carefully cultivated. It is earned over time as the organisation learns to understand both itself and its **stakeholders**. Good reputations can be lost far more easily than they can be earned.

See **public relations, relationship management.**

Research

Research is the systematic collection and interpretation of information and data. In the field of **public relations**, practitioners must acquire a great deal of relevant and accurate data about their **publics**, products, programmes and competitors. In 1997, the Institute for Public Relations Research and Education suggested seven guiding principles in setting standards for **public relations** research:

1 Clear programme **objectives** and desired outcomes should be established and should mirror business goals.
2 The measurement of **public relations outputs** (e.g. the amount of press coverage acquired) and **public relations outcomes** (e.g. changing awareness) should be differentiated.
3 The measurement of media content should only be taken as a first step in research. There is no proof that an **audience** actually sees or responds to it.
4 It should be understood that no single research method can be used to evaluate **public relations** effectively. A series of research methods should be used, both **qualitative research methods** and **quantitative research methods**.
5 The more an organisation has researched its identification of **audience**s, key **messages** and desired channels of communication, the more reliable its **public relations** management will be.

There are two types of **public relations** research: applied and theoretical. Applied research falls into two categories:

- *Strategic* research is used primarily in programme development to determine programme **objectives**, develop **messages** or establish benchmarks. It often examines the **tools** or **techniques** of **public relations**.
- *Evaluative* research is used primarily to determine whether a **public relations programme/plan** has realised its goals and **objectives**.

Theoretical research is more abstract and conceptual than applied research. It explores the theoretical considerations of **public relations** and examines how **public opinion** is formed and how/why people communicate.

> *See* **analysis, evaluation, focus groups, qualitative research methods, quantitative research methods.**

Resistance

Advertisers and **public relations** practitioners aim to reinforce customers so that they will continue their buying behaviour with them. One form of reinforcement is termed 'resistance'. Here sellers attempt to strengthen existing **attitudes** so that customers will resist the persuasive **messages** sent by others (competitors), which may attempt to change these **attitudes**. William McGuire (1964) developed an important theory of resistance which he termed **inoculation theory**.

See **attitudes, beliefs, persuasion, resistance, values.**

McGuire, W. J. (1964) 'Inducing resistance in persuasion: Some contemporary approaches', in L. Berkowitz (ed.) *Advances in Experimental Social Psychology*, vol. 1, 191–229. New York: Academic Press.

Resources

Resources for **public relations** campaigns come under three headings:

* human resources
* **operating costs**
* equipment.

Human resources depend on the size and nature of the **public relations programme/plan** and include items such as salaries, overheads and expenses. Operating costs need to consider both the effectiveness and the efficiency of the campaign and can include all costs from print and production to the cost of media **conferences**. Equipment includes costs for such things as office furniture, computer equipment and consumables.

See **advisory fees, implementation fees.**

Reuters

Reuters is a financial market data provider and news service which provides reports from around the world to newspapers and broadcasters. Reuters has a team of several thousand **journalist**s who have covered major news events.

See **external media support.**

www.reuters.com

Review (consumer)

A consumer review is a review written by the owner of a product or the user of a service who will comment on whether the product or service has delivered its promises.

Review (media)

A media review is an **evaluation** of a publication or broadcast or software.

Review (public relations)

In **public relations** written copy will frequently be reviewed by an independent public relations practitioner in order to check the facts before publication. This is one reason why **public relations** stories are often more factually reliable than stories produced by the mass media. However 'fact-based' **public relations** stories must still be newsworthy and interesting enough to appeal to a mass **audience**.

Rhetoric

Rhetoric studies the use of effective language **techniques** and the art of using speech to persuade and influence. Rhetoric plays a part in mass communications, including **marketing, advertising** and **public relations**.

See **Aristotle, influence (laws of), persuasion.**

Rhetorical questions

Rhetorical questions are questions which are intended to be answered by the speaker and not the listener, or sometimes are not meant to be answered explicitly at all. They may be expressive of the speaker's epistemic state. Rhetorical questions have a long tradition in **public speaking**. **Aristotle** argues, in his book *The Art of Rhetoric* (c. 330BC), that rhetorical questions weaken an opposing argument if used as part of the conclusion of a speech. They are used in arguments today as a method of **persuasion** and cognitively to engage the recipient of the communication with the **message**.

See **questionnaires.**

Risk

According to Regester and Larkin (2005, 38) 'a *risk* is a measure of the adverse affect of an issue. It is about assessing and communicating the possible hazards associated with a particular process relative to the safeguards and benefits which it offers.' This allows consumers to make choices about their health and safety and the

R

protection of the environment. Regester and Larkin suggest that risk assessment is essential when:

- a new risk emerges;
- the degree of risk changes;
- a new perception of risk occurs.

A simple matrix, with axes depicting the degree of threat against the probability of occurrence, is commonly used to categorise risks and then prioritise remedial actions (see Figure 30).

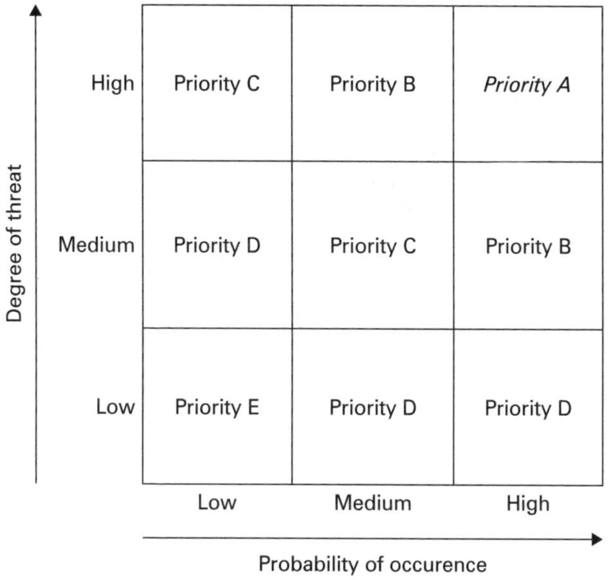

	Low	Medium	High
High	Priority C	Priority B	*Priority A*
Medium	Priority D	Priority C	Priority B
Low	Priority E	Priority D	Priority D

Degree of threat (vertical axis) — Probability of occurence (horizontal axis)

Figure 30   Risk assessment matrix
Source: Swartz and Herbane (2002)

R

Although risk assessment appears to be based on statistical calculation, this is not the case, as emotion, cultural context and power all play a role. Some risks may be actual; others may be perceptions manufactured through individual sense-making and judgements. Whatever the genesis of the risk, risk and risk debates make juicy copy for **journalist**s who wish to write gloom-and-doom **headlines**.

Regester, M. and Larkin, J. (2005) *Risk Issues and Crisis Management, a Casebook of Best Practice*, 3rd edn. London: Kogan Page.
Smith, D. and Elliott, D. (eds) (2006) *Key Readings in Crisis Management, Systems and Structures for Prevention and Recovery*. Abingdon: Routledge.

See **crisis management, issues management, risk.**

ROPES

ROPES stands for:

- <u>R</u>**esearch**
- <u>O</u>**bjectives**
- <u>P</u>rogramming
- <u>E</u>**valuation**
- <u>S</u>tewardship.

ROPES provides a comprehensive theory of **relationship management**. Figure 31 explains this process.

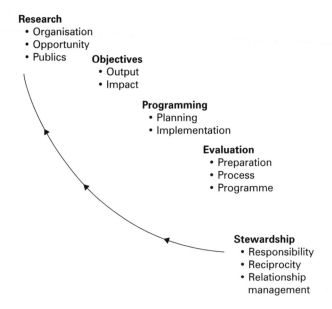

Figure 31   The ROPES process

The **public relations** process starts with **research** in three areas:

1 the organisation itself;
2 the problem, **issue** or opportunity faced by the organisation;
3 the **publics** and **stakeholders** involved in the problem, **issue** or opportunity.

The second step is to set measurable **objectives**. Output **objectives** deal with the **public relations tools** or **techniques**. Impact **objectives** deal with the intended effects of the programme.

The third step, programming, consists of implementing activities designed to bring about the outcomes in the **objectives**. **Evaluation** is conducted in three areas, **messages** and **techniques** are tested (preparation **evaluation**), programming is monitored and adjusted (process) and results are measured and compared to set **objectives**. Finally, stewardship leads back to the beginning of the loop by a process of **relationship management**.

Routes to persuasion

Petty and Cacioppo (1986) suggest that there are two routes to persuasion. The first they term the *central route to persuasion*. This occurs when a listener thinks carefully about the content of the **message** and its argument. The listener needs both motivation and time in order to be able to do this. Thoughts and cognitive responses are produced during this period of central processing. The basis of **persuasion** in central processing is the strength and quality of the argument in the message. The *peripheral route to persuasion* takes place when receivers do not think very carefully or too hard about the message. Instead they take clues about its credibility from other sources, for example whether the message sender is an expert or is particularly knowledgeable in his/her field. These peripheral cues act as a 'mental short-cut'. Receivers engaged in peripheral processing are therefore more passive than those centrally processing.

See **attitudes, cognitive dissonance, cognitive response model, persuasion.**

Petty R. E. and Cacioppo J. T. (1986) *Communication and Persuasion: Central and Peripheral Routes to Attitude Change.* New York: Springer-Verlag.

R

Ss

Sapir-Whorf hypothesis

The Sapir-Whorf hypothesis, also known as the 'linguistic relativity hypothesis', postulates that language structures consciousness. The hypothesis suggests that a particular language's nature influences the habitual thoughts of its speakers and that different language patterns yield different patterns of thought. Edward Sapir held that language does not merely mirror culture and habitual action, that language and thought are in a relationship of mutual influence. Language and its use is therefore an important concept for **public relations** practitioners to consider when aiming to change people's **attitudes** about a product or service.

See **gatekeeper.**

Lacey, J. A. (1992) *Language Diversity and Thought: A Reformulation of the Linguistic Relativity Hypothesis*. Cambridge: Cambridge University Press.

Scripts

Scripts can be divided into those for:

- film
- radio
- speeches
- television
- **DVDs**
- on-line.

Film scripts are written for films and **DVDs** made to be shown to employees, at community meetings, schools and colleges, events, **exhibitions**, museums and other display areas. Films can be made to promote, to persuade, to inform, to entertain or to trigger important debates. Films are known as passive media and work well with people with low involvement. Careful **research** and planning must be done before film is chosen as the main medium of communication. Films require time and resource **budget**ing. Scripting for film begins as a general idea for which a synopsis or summary is then written in the present tense. This synopsis should indicate the style, mood and overall theme of the film. Once the synopsis is approved, a treatment must then be written. The treatment is a scene-by-scene explanation of everything which will happen in the film. Both the synopsis and the treatment are planning **tools** which enable the **public relations** practitioner to visualise the film. When the treatment is approved, the script and **storyboard** will then be written, complete with camera directions, times and dialogue.

Secondary research

Secondary research is often referred to as desk **research**. It entails collecting information from previously established and published sources. Vast collections of published material are archived on-line and can be accessed from library and university **databases**; these are linked to international information **databases**. The internet also holds huge reserves of information, as does the archived material belonging to specific organisations. The large **research** companies such as **Mintel, Mori** and Gallup conduct their own surveys on various subjects and their material can be purchased either as hard copy or on-line.

> www.ipsos-mori.com
> www.mintel.com

Seeding content

The term 'seeding content' refers to a **public relations** practitioner's attempts to 'seed in' or place **public relations** information into an on-line forum. If done covertly, there are obvious ethical implications.

> *See* **properties and product placement.**

S

Segmentation

Segmentation (or market segmentation) refers to groups of people or organisations which share one or more characteristics, which causes them to have similar products needs. Broadly, markets can be divided according to a number of criteria or variables such as **demographic**, geographic, attitudinal or behavioural data. Smaller markets are often termed niche markets or speciality markets. Knowing an organisation's markets leads to increased effectiveness, productivity and customer satisfaction.

The general variables used for segmentation are as follows:

- *geographic*: region of the world or country, country size, density or rural or urban living, climate;
- *demographic*: age, gender, family size, family life cycle, education, income, occupation, socio-economic status, religion, nationality, race, language;
- *psychographic*: personality, lifestyle, **values**, **attitudes**;
- *behavioural*: benefit sought, product usage rate, **brand** loyalty, product end use, readiness-to-buy stage, decision-making unit, profitability.

See **demographics.**

Semiotics

Semiotics is a vast field of study originating in the study of language and pioneered by Ferdinand de Saussure (1916), a few elements of which are relevant to students of **public relations**. Semiotics is concerned with how meaning is constructed in the mind of the receiver of a message. It argues that receivers decode words and images according to their own personal, cultural, and social references. In essence this means that individuals create their own meanings of a message. Saussure proposed that a sign is made up of the physical reality of the thing (the signifier) and the mental concept that the decoder holds of the thing (the signified). He also suggested that the signified is distinguished as much by what it is not as by what it is. For example a woman is a not-man and a not-girl. Meanings gathered in this way reflect the **values** and culture of the decoder.

In semiotics meanings can be described as:

- *denotative*: the literal meaning of the word as found in the dictionary, e.g. car – a self-propelled vehicle designed to carry passengers;
- *connotative*: the images and associations created in the mind of the receiver, e.g. the office can be a place of exciting activity or a place of boredom;
- *ambiguous*: where the same word can mean different things in the same language, e.g. right can mean the opposite of left or it can mean correct. In **copywriting** and **advertising**, puns make use of ambiguous words for effect;
- *polysemic*: where the same readers/viewers gain different meanings from the same set of information, e.g. a photograph

of a war zone may represent different meanings to people of different cultures or different ideological or political leanings.

Semiotics makes **public relations** practitioners think about how people use the information they encode to construct their own meanings. It reminds practitioners not to assume that all people share the same views and ideologies and prevents offence.

Chandler, D. (2007) *Semiotics: The Basics*. Abingdon: Routledge.

Saussure, F. de (1916) *Cours de linguistique générale,* ed. C. Bally and A. Schehaye. Lausanne and Paris: Payot, trans. W. Baskin (1977) *Course in General Linguistics*. Glasgow: Fontana/Collins.

Seven Cs of communication

Cutlip *et al.* (1994) present seven useful guidelines for effective communication:

1 *Credibility*: the communication source must be credible. Communication is built upon a climate of **belief** and the receiver must have confidence in the source's competence on the subject.
2 *Context*: the communication programme must provide a context for participation and must confirm and not contradict the **message**.
3 *Content*: the message must have meaning for the receiver and must be compatible with his/her value system. The content determines the **audience**.
4 *Clarity*: the message must be clear, simple and easily understood.
5 *Continuity and consistency*: communication is never-ending and requires repetition of **messages** to achieve penetration.
6 *Channels*: different channels should be used for reaching different target **audience**s. Different channels are associated with different **values** and this should be considered by the **public relations** practitioner.
7 *Capability of the **audience***: communication is most effective when it requires the least amount of hard work by the recipient, so the capabilities of the **audience** must also be considered.

Cutlip, S. M. Center, A. H. and Broom, G. M. (1994) *Effective Public Relations,* 7th edn. Englewood Cliffs, NJ: Prentice Hall.

S

Shannon and Weaver

See **communication theory.**

Show reels

Show reels are also known as video **pitch**es. They are used by **public relations** organisations, **advertising** agencies and other service organisations when **pitch**ing to potential clients.

Single-issue publics

Single-issue publics are a subset of **active publics** as defined by James **Grunig**. Single-issue publics are active on one **issue** or on a small set of **issue**s. They might not be opposed to the organisation outright but to just one particular **issue** that the organisation may be experiencing.

> See **Grunig's four models of public relations, publics.**

Situation analysis

Any **public relations programme/plan** cannot be planned without an **analysis** of the organisational situation. A situation analysis will include both a **communications audit** and an **image** audit and will consider the following variables:

- **market research** to understand the state of public awareness about the organisation;
- an **image study**;
- desk **research** analysing the organisation's **annual report** and accounts, policy, prospects and performance;
- the complaints procedures and outcomes;
- **media attitudes** to the organisation;
- employee management relations;
- **community relations**.

> See **PEST analysis, SWOT analysis.**

Situational theory of publics

The situational theory of **publics** was developed by James **Grunig** in 1984. The theory suggests that **publics** can be identified and classified by the situation in which they find themselves, i.e. if publics know of a pre-existing problem or issue which has the potential to affect them in some way, then they may (or may not) seek to act on the issue or problem. The theory outlines when communications are most likely to be effective because it addresses a **public**'s understanding and cognition of an **issue** in terms of a group's information-seeking and processing behaviour. The following key concepts are variables within the theory:

- **Problem recognition**: this is the extent to which individuals recognise that they have a problem. People generally do not realise that there is a problem unless they perceive that something needs to be done about a situation to improve it.
- **Constraint recognition**: this is the extent to which individuals perceive their actions to be limited by factors beyond their control. This could range from low self-esteem to lack of finances.
- *Level of involvement*: this is the extent to which people are emotionally and personally involved in a problem. Involvement increases the chances of individuals listening to and understanding **messages**.
- *Information-seeking*: information-seeking is also termed 'active communication behaviour'. These **publics** actively communicate, seek out information and try to understand it. **Publics** who seek out information become **aware publics** more often than those **publics** who only process information or those who do not communicate at all.
- *Information-processing*: information-processing is also termed 'passive communication behaviour'. These **publics** will not seek out information but may passively process random communications.

See **Grunig (James), publics.**

Grunig, J. (1997) 'A situational theory of publics: Conceptual history, recent challenges and new research', in D. Moss, T. MacManus and D. Vercic (eds) *Public Relations Research: An International Perspective*. London: International Thomson Business Press, 3–48.

Slander

Slander is a harmful statement in a transitory form, especially speech.

See **defamation, libel.**

Slogans

Slogan are usually written by **advertising copywriters** and should be a statement of merit about a product or a service which is worthy of continuous repetition and is phrased in such a memorable way that the public is likely to remember it and associate it with the product or service without thinking too hard about it. Slogans should:

- be memorable;
- recall the **brand** name;
- include a key benefit;
- differentiate the **brand**;
- impart positive feelings for the **brand**;
- reflect the **brand**'s personality;
- be strategic;
- be competitive;
- be original;
- be simple;
- be believable.

Slogans should NOT:

- be in current use by others;
- be bland, generic or hackneyed;
- prompt a sarcastic or negative response;
- be pretentious;
- be corporate **spin**;
- be meaningless.

Furthermore, great slogans should beg to be chanted, use as few words as possible and create vivid pictures in the minds of their **audience**. The slogan voted no. 1 by the Advertising Slogan Hall of Fame is 'Beanz means Heinz'.

See **jingle.**

www.adslogans.co.uk

Slug word

The slug word is the header at the top right-hand side of the second page of a **press release**. It is used as a means of identifying pages if they become separated. The word chosen to act as the slug should be selected from the first paragraph of the story and should be a key to the most important factor of the news.

Small-group communication

Small-group communication refers to the study of group dynamics. It involves the **analysis** of the nature of groups, the laws of their development and their interrelations with individuals, other groups and larger institutions. Small groups are classified on the basis of the reason they were formed and the human needs they serve.

Primary groups satisfy needs for love and belonging and include:

- families
- social groups
- close friends
- activity groups
- learning groups (study, interest groups).

Secondary groups satisfy needs for control and power and include:

- therapy and self-help groups
- problem-solving groups
- committees
- task forces
- conference groups
- quality circles
- production teams
- self-managed work teams
- work crews.

Public relations practitioners are more interested in the way in which secondary groups communicate and how they are able to inform, persuade or **influence** them.

Brilhart, J. K. and Galanes, G. J. (1995) *Effective Group Discussion*, 8th edn. WCB Brown and Benchmark: Dubuque, IA.

SMART

SMART is an acronym and relates to the setting of **objectives** which should be:

- Specific
- Measurable
- Achievable
- Realistic
- Timebound.

See **objectives.**

Snooze news

As every **public relations** practitioner knows – news should be newsworthy. 'Snooze news' is the term given to stories that **public relations** practitioners feel should make the **headlines**, but in reality send **journalist**s to sleep.

Social exchange theory

Good **relationship-building** and maintenance induces collaboration and produces a **win–win** situation for resolving conflict. Known as social exchange theory, this concept proves to be more effective in producing change within organisations, their **stakeholders** and **publics** than confrontation. Grunig, Grunig and Ehling (1992) identified six variables which they considered to be the most effective constituents of a positive relationship:

1 reciprocity
2 trust
3 credibility
4 mutual legitimacy
5 openness
6 mutual satisfaction and understanding.

Grunig, L. A., Grunig, J. E. and Ehling, W. P. (1992) 'What is an effective organisation?', in J. E. Grunig *et al.* (eds), *Excellence in Public Relations and Communications Management*. Hillsdale, NJ: Lawrence Erlbaum, 65–90.

Social marketing

Social marketing acts as a force for change at local, regional, national and global levels. It segments mass **audience**s on the basis of **demographics**, geography, **psychographics**, **attitudes** and behaviour. Social marketing includes the following:

- Social **advertising** campaigns
- Social **market research**
- Social communication
- Social product development

It is based on **quantitative research** and the **objectives** are much the same as those of **public relations**, that is measurable and about changes in behaviour. Social marketing adapts commercial concepts and thinking to the field of health, personal empowerment and other sensitive **issue**s.

Social media

Social media is an umbrella term for activities incorporating the use of technology and social interaction. Social media can include:

- internet forums
- **message** boards

- **weblogs**
- **wikis**
- **podcast**s
- pictures
- video
- twitters.

Examples of social media applications are MySpace, Facebook and YouTube for social **networking**, Google and Wikipedia for reference, Last.fm for personal music, Second Life for virtual reality and Flickr for photo-sharing.

Dijk, J. van (2006) *The Network Society: Social Aspects of New Media*, 2nd edn. London: Sage.

SOLAADS

See **press release.**

Soundbites

Soundbites are short sentences or phrases which deftly captures the essence of what the speaker is trying to say. Usually memorable, they are used to summarise large amounts of information. Soundbites are used and liked by news media and politicians as they focus on dialogue which helps to advance the overall nub of the message. An example of a memorable soundbite is one spoken by Tony Blair following the 1998 Good Friday Agreement: 'I feel the hand of history upon our shoulders.'

See **copywriting, messages, rhetoric.**

Spamming

Spamming is the abuse of electronic messaging systems to send unsolicited bulk messages indiscriminately. Spamming, unethical as it is, is considered economically viable because advertisers have limited **operating costs**. It is also difficult to hold senders accountable for their mass mailings.

Span of control

Span of control relates to the number of subordinates who report directly to a single manager or supervisor within an organisation.

See **hierarchy, organisational chart, organisational structure, organisational structure of public relations.**

Speech-writing/speech-making

Speech-writing is one of the **techniques** or **tools** used by **public relations** practitioners to communicate **messages**. Speeches are designed to persuade others to a route of action or thought and use **rhetoric** to achieve this. Speech is a useful means of **persuasion** because it is flexible and can be altered to fit the response of the **audience**. Adequate planning must precede speech-writing. The writer must ascertain what type of **audience** is being addressed and what its needs are. The speech must be reviewed comprehensively before it 'goes live'. The speech-writer must have access to the speaker in order to ensure that the speech has the desired impact, and lastly the speech must be rehearsed. Like other **public relations messages**, speeches should be consistent with the other **messages** disseminated by the organisation. Simple tips for speech-writing include:

- Find out what the speaker wants to say.
- Know the **audience**.
- Write a strong opening.
- Consider humour.
- Don't try to cover too much.
- Write in a conversational tone.
- Keep it simple.
- Consider visuals.
- Consider handouts.
- Write a catchy title

Other **issue**s to consider are:

- Is a speech the best forum for reaching the target **audience**?
- Will it help the organisation achieve its goals?
- Is a speech making best use of the **resources**?
- Should the speech be reinforced with other channels of communication?
- Will the effect be measurable?

The majority of speeches follow the three-rule principle of introduction–body–conclusion, although some do deviate. There are a number of recognised 'attention-getters' which speech-writers use to stimulate the **audience**:

- Report a startling statement or statistic.
- Ask a question.
- Use a quotation.
- Refer to the **audience** or the speaking situation.
- Use an analogy.

S

- Tell a story.
- Talk about a personal experience.

If the reason for the speech is to problem-solve, the following problem-solution outline (based on Benoit and Benoit, 2008) should be used.

Introduction

1. Use an attention-getter.
2. Establish a rapport.
3. Give the **audience** a reason to listen.
4. State the purpose.
5. Preview the main points.

Body

1. Main point (statement of problem)
   - Subpoint (cause of problem)
   - Subpoint (effect of problem)
   - Subpoint (problem will continue)
2. Main point (statement of solution)
   - Subpoint (solution will address the cause of problem)
   - Subpoint (solution will work)
   - Subpoint (solution is the best of all possible options).

Conclusion

1. Summary
2. Connection
3. Cohesive element
4. Appropriate frame of mind
5. Final appeal.

See **persuasion.**

Benoit, W. L. and Benoit, P. (2008) *Persuasive Messages: The Process of Influence*. Oxford: Blackwell.

S

Spin

Spin is a pejorative term meaning a biased portrayal in one's own favour to support a personal agenda, an event or a situation. Spin often implies deceptive or manipulative **tactics** and those accused of working in this way are termed 'spin doctors'. It is a term increasingly used in the world of party politics. Some of the **techniques** of **spin** include:

- using facts selectively (cherry-picking);
- using euphemisms to promote one's own cause;

- phrasing facts in such a way that they are assumed to be true;
- delaying the release of bad news until a more important event overshadows it.

Genasi, C. (2002) *Winning Reputations: How to Be your own Spin Doctor*. Basingstoke: Palgrave.
Miller, D. and Dinan, W. (2008) *A Century of Spin: How Public Relations Became the Cutting Edge of Corporate Power*. London: Pluto.

Spokespeople

Spokespeople are those people who speak to the media and **stakeholders** on behalf of an organisation, especially in a **crisis** situation.

Sponsorship

The primary objective of sponsorship is generally a strategic **marketing** investment. Most sponsors are investors who wish to see a direct return on their **brand** equity and increased sales. There are two elements to sponsorship:

1 those seeking funds;
2 those wishing to engage in sponsorship.

It is vitally important to match the sponsor and sponsee appropriately in order to obtain a **win–win** situation for both parties. BDS Sponsorship (2005) defines sponsorship as 'a business relationship between a provider of funds, **resources** or services and an individual, event or organisation which offers in return some rights and association that may be used for commercial advantage in return for sponsorship advantage'. Figure 32 illustrates the sponsorship **audience**, outlining the potential overlap.

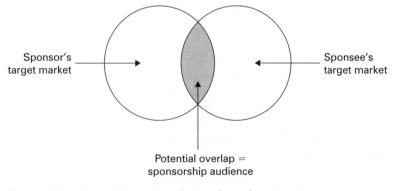

Sponsor's target market → ← Sponsee's target market

Potential overlap = sponsorship audience

Figure 32   Potential overlap for a **win–win** situation

There are a number of reasons for **public relations** professionals to engage in sponsorship. These can include:

- *Corporate image* and *identity*: an organisation can promote its **image**, house colour, typography, livery and any other physical manifestations.
- *Audience* *awareness*: sponsorship allows the sponsor repetition of its **brand** with associations to the sponsee. It is also a method of gaining entry into a foreign market.
- *Employee and customer relations*: employees may take pride in the associations with the sponsor; it may act as a morale booster.
- *Media coverage*: media coverage may be extensive and act as a **brand**ing exercise.

Sponsorship generally falls into four types:

1 entertainment
2 the arts
3 sport
4 social causes.

Table 12 details the characteristics of each type of sponsorship.

Fry, A. (2001) 'How to profit from sponsoring sport', *Marketing*, 16 Aug., 25–26.

Table 12 Sponsorship types and their characteristics

Type of sponsorship	Associated properties	Type of audience	Size of audience	Reasons for sponsorship
Entertainment	Progressive and established	Dependent on genre of entertainment	Mass	Market penetration
The arts	Creativity and excellence	Exclusive	Niche	Niche market development
Sport	Competitive, dynamicss	Youth, young adults	Large, possibly global	International market development
Social causes	Socially concerned	Community-based, sometimes local, regional, national or international	Variable	**Image** and market development

S

Stakeholders

An organisation's **stakeholders** are those **publics** who have an interest in the organisation. The most important to the **public relations** practitioner are the key players – those individuals or groups who have the power to affect organisational policy. However, any effective **public relations programme/plan** should communicate with all the organisation's **stakeholders**.

See **publics, stakeholder model.**

Stakeholder model

The stakeholder model is a Kantian approach which argues that the task of the **public relations** practitioner or communications manager is to balance the needs and interests of all the groups who have a 'stake' in the organisation, including the shareholders, customers, suppliers and employees, the local community and the wider society in general. The model requires the organisation to account for its social responsibilities.

See **corporate social responsibility.**

Storyboard

Storyboards are drawn to accompany **scripts** for short **promotion**al films, **DVDs** and adverts (see Figure 33). The storyboard itself enables the film-maker to present a visual representation of the story to the **public relations** manager early in the planning process. A storyboard is made up of individual sketches, each representing a frame or film sequence in a picture-book style. The main images are drawn on to the blank screens and the words go underneath. These frames indicate the movements and relationships of the characters and objects involved.

Readman, M. (2003) *Teaching Scriptwriting, Screenplays and Storyboards for Film and TV Production.* London: BFI.

Strategic planning

The strategic function of any organisation should contribute to its overall **mission** and goals. The strategic function of **public relations** occurs when the efforts contribute to the success of the organisation. In **public relations** terms, success can mean the bottom line and/or the organisation's contributions to its community

S

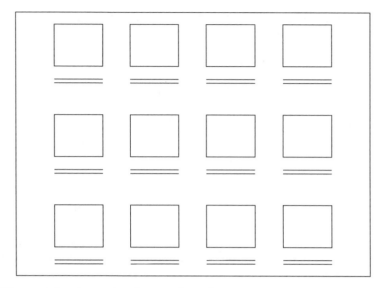

Figure 33 Example of a storyboard

or diverse **publics**. The highly competitive business environment today places a responsibility on all organisations to be accountable for their actions. Strategic planning involves the move away from the basic 'research, plan, implement, evaluate' model to something more strategic, such as:

- devising an organisationally strategic plan which responds to and incorporates information from **research**;
- creating **tactics** which succeed in accomplishing what the plan identifies needs to be done to support the organisation's mission and goals.

Laurie Wilson (1997) suggests the following steps for strategic programme planning for effective public relations:

- **Research**
  - *Background*: the synthesis of **primary research** and **secondary research** providing background information on the industry and client, the product or programme, market situation and current trends in opinion and **attitudes**.
  - *Situation analysis*: a one-paragraph statement of the current situation and a definition of the problem based on

S

research; a second paragraph identifies potential difficulties and related problems to be considered.

- *Central core of difficulty*: a one-sentence statement outlining the heart of the problem and the potential harm to the client if it is not resolved.
- *Preliminary identification of* **publics** *and* **resources**: an identification in two parts – the first part identifies and profiles all potential **publics** who may be affected by the problem or need to be motivated to aid its resolution; the second part identifies the **intervening publics** and other **resources** (both tangible and intangible) who can be drawn on for the campaign.
- *Campaign goals*: the end to be achieved to resolve the central core of difficulty.
- ***Objectives***: specific, measurable, achievable, realistic and time-bound **objectives** which will help achievement of the campaign goals.
- *Key* **publics**: those **audience**s necessary to achieve the campaign **objectives** and goals. The **research** assesses current relationships with each set of **publics** and identifies those who will influence others in their community.
- Planning
- *Message design*: identifies the primary and secondary **messages** for each key public, incorporating **messages** which serve each key **public's** self-interest.
  - *Strategies*: identifies specific strategies for each public designed to reach that public with its specially designed **messages**.
  - *Tactics*: specifies **tactics** or media **tools** to support each **strategy** for each specific public. Each **strategy** will need to be supported with a number of **tactics** designed to convey the message to that public through the channel designated by the **strategy**.
  - *Calendar*: a time-task matrix such as a **Gantt chart** or **critical path analysis** to integrate implementation of the strategic plan. The matrix should be organised by each public and **strategy**, scheduling each **tactic**.
  - ***Budget***: the budget should consider differing publics and the strategies needed to communicate with them and should project the cost of each tactic in specific terms. It should also indicate where costs could be offset by donations or **sponsorship**.

S

- Communication
  - *Communication confirmation*: Table 13 converts the plan devised for each public into short words in tabular form, and the strategies and **tactics** for each public are reviewed to ensure that they are appropriate. The table provides verification of the analytical processes to ensure that the plan will reach the intended **publics** with the **messages** which will motivate them to action such that the campaign goals will be accomplished.

Table 13 Communication confirmation table

Key public	Self-interests	Influentials	Strategy	Tactics/tools	Message
1.					
2.					
3.					

Evaluation

- *Evaluation criteria*: specific criteria to measure success, based on the campaign goals and **objectives**.
- *Evaluation tools*: specific **evaluation tools** appropriate to measure each of the **evaluation** criteria, including those in the calendar and **budget**.

Wilson, L. J. (1997) *Strategic Program Planning for Effective Public Relations Campaigns*, 2nd edn. Dubuque, IA: Kendall Hunt.

S

Strategy

Strategy is a major part of any **public relations programme/plan**. It describes 'how the organisation is going to get where it wants to go and differs from **objectives** and **tactics**. Put simply:

- *Objectives* are where the organisation wants to go.
- *Strategies* are how the organisation is going to get there.
- *Tactics* are the operational aspects of the strategy.

Oliver, S. (2007) *Public Relations Strategy*, 2nd edn. London: Kogan Page.

SWOT analysis

SWOT is an acronym for:

- Strengths
- Weaknesses
- Opportunities
- Threats.

A SWOT analysis is a framework for reviewing an organisation's:

- position
- **strategy**
- direction
- ideas.

A SWOT analysis organises the subjective assessment of data into a logical format which helps understanding, presentation, discussion and decision-making. Table 14 suggests some headings which could be considered, using a SWOT analysis.

Table 14   Suggested headings for a SWOT analysis

Strengths	Weaknesses
Competitive advantages	Gaps in capabilities
USPs	Lack of competitive strength
Resources, assets, people	Reputation, presence and reach
Experience, knowledge	Financial weaknesses
Financial reserves	Own known vulnerabilities
Marketing – reach, distribution, awareness	**Timescales**, deadlines and pressures
Innovative aspects	Cash flow, start-up cash drain
Location	Supply chain robustness
Price, quality, value	Morale, commitment, leadership
Accreditations, qualifications, certifications	Processes and systems
Processes, systems, ITC	Succession, management cover
Cultural, attitudinal, behavioural strengths	
Succession, management cover	

(Continued)

Table 14 Continued

Opportunities	Threats
Market developments	Political effects
Competitor's vulnerabilities	Legislative effects
Industry or lifestyle trends	Environmental effects
Technology development	Technology developments
New markets	Competitor intentions
Niche target markets	Market demand
New USPs	Sustaining internal capabilities
Tactics	Loss of key staff
Major **contracts**	Crises
Product and development	Economy – home and abroad
Information and **research**	Seasonality and weather effects
Partnerships	
Volumes, production, economies	
Seasonal, weather, fashion influences	

A SWOT analysis can be used to assess:

- an organisation's position in the market and commercial viability
- a method of sales distribution
- a product or **brand**
- a business idea
- a strategic option
- a potential partnership
- a supplier change
- an outsourcing of a service
- an investment opportunity.

A **PEST analysis** helps to identify SWOT factors and there is often an overlap between the two in that similar factors would appear in each. However, a **PEST analysis** and a SWOT analysis are different perspectives, analysing macro and micro environments respectively.

See **analysis, PEST analysis, research.**

S

Symmetrical communication

The premise of symmetrical communication is that it should lead to a **win–win** situation between an organisation and its **publics**. Symmetrical communication should involve:

- interdependence with other systems in the environment (see **systems theory**);
- free exchange of information across boundaries;
- moving equilibrium with other organisations.

Communication leads to understanding, and so symmetrical communication offers:

- equal opportunities and respect for members of the organisation (equity);
- a degree of power over individual tasks linked to job satisfaction (autonomy);
- the privileging of new ideas over tradition (innovation);
- the decentralisation of management to enable increased autonomy and employee satisfaction;
- social responsibility;
- **conflict resolution** through **negotiation**, communication and compromise;
- interest-group liberalism.

See **asymmetrical communication, Grunig's four models of public relations.**

Systems theory

Public relations are a system. Systems require the concepts of input, throughput and output to exist. **Public relations** systems receive inputs from the environment in the form of information. These inputs can identify problems which have upset the equilibrium between the system and other interdependent systems in its environment. Systems process these inputs (a process known as throughput) to release outputs (or solutions to the problems). After the outputs affect the environment, the system then seeks **feedback** from the environment to determine if it has solved the problem that it first identified. This process resumes until the original equilibrium is restored (see Figure 34).

A *reactive* system changes only when the environment forces it to do so. A *proactive* system tries to change other systems in its environment, even if the equilibrium between the interdependent systems has not been upset.

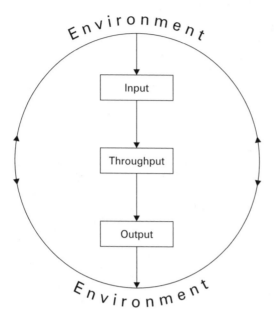

Figure 34   Systems theory

Proactive behaviour begins with the throughputs rather than the inputs. The proactive organisation releases throughputs which will affect the interdependent systems. The resulting outputs upset the equilibrium of these interdependent systems and their reaction produces a problem for the organisation which initiated the outputs. It must then manage the new inputs which arrive from the interdependent systems which are seeking to restore equilibrium. Put simply, in order to bring about change, organisations may purposely do things which affect their environment. For example, if a supermarket wishes to buy up land to build another supermarket, it must realise that its actions will bring it into conflict with environmental groups who are trying to preserve the land. When the environmental groups object to the consequences of the land buy-out, they create a **public relations** problem for the supermarket. The supermarket must then deal with the problem in order to restore the equilibrium between the interdependent systems.

See **open system.**

S

Tactics

Tactics, also known as **tools**, are a set of **techniques** for achieving the **public relations objectives.** In the planning cycle, tactics come after the **objectives** and the **strategy**. Different campaigns need different tactics, and different **publics** respond differently to a given set of tactics. It is therefore important to make sure that the tactics chosen are appropriate to the targeted **audience**. The tactics are **tools** of **influence** and **persuasion** and are important communication activities for the **public relations** practitioner to consider. Tactics have weaknesses as well as strengths, and an efficacious communications programme should select a range of **techniques** which complement each other and which, taken together, offer a potent set of **messages**.

Tactics must be:

- appropriate to the target group;
- deliverable.

A small selection of possible **public relations** tactics are shown below:

- **press conference**s
- **news release**s
- photo calls
- briefings, one-to-one briefings
- **articles** and features
- interviews
- receptions
- photography
- **advertising**
- trade **exhibitions**, public **exhibitions**
- **website**s, e-mail, **blog**s, **intranet**
- multimedia material
- corporate literature, **Annual Report**s, **brochures**
- background briefings and materials

- posters, flyers, leaflets, **newsletter**s, **direct mail**
- CDs, **DVDs**
- **sponsorship**, donations, **hospitality**, gifts in kind
- **Annual General Meeting**s **(AGMs)**, Special General Meetings
- launches, **competitions, publicity stunts**
- **corporate image** design
- merchandising.

Gregory, A. (2004) *Planning and Managing Public Relations Campaigns*, 2nd edn. London: Kogan Page.

Tallents (Sir Stephen)

Sir Stephen Tallents (1884–1958) was a writer, philanthropist, the founder of **public relations** in Britain and arguably the world's first multi-media entrepreneur. Between 1926 and 1933 he was the secretary of the Empire Marketing Board (EMB) where he specialised in promoting awareness of the British Empire through an innovative programme of press and poster campaigns, **exhibitions**, shops and radio broadcasts. With the demise of the EMB he was appointed **public relations** officer for the GPO where he devised a series of ground- breaking **marketing** and **advertising** campaigns. Tallent's later career took him to the **BBC** and the Ministry of Information. After the Second World War he became the founder president of the Institute of Public Relations.

Task-oriented structure

See **organisational structure of public relations.**

Technician

The **public relations** or **communication technician** is not involved in the decision-making process. Technicians implement the tactical parts of the **public relations programme/plan**, such as writing the **feature articles, press release**s and web content. They are answerable to the **public relations** manager.

See **public relations, Public Relations Consultants Association (PRCA).**

Techniques

See **task-oriented structure, tools.**

T

Teleconference

A teleconference is the live exchange of information among individuals and machines who are remote but linked via a telecommunications system. Both teleconferencing and **videoconferencing** are useful **tools** for **public relations** practitioners.

Telemarketing

Telemarketing is a means of direct **marketing** by which the salesperson relies on the telephone as the channel of communication. Telemarketing is used to solicit prospective customers to buy products or services over the phone. Telemarketing can be done from an office, a call centre or a home. Charities, alumni associations and political parties often use telemarketing to solicit donations. Telemarketing is considered an annoyance by many on the receiving end but telemarketing is subject to regulatory and legislative controls related to privacy and protection. The two categories of telemarketing are **business to business (B2B)** and **business to consumer (B2C)**, and subcategories include:

- *lead generation*: where information is gathered;
- *sales*: where **persuasion** is used to sell a product or service;
- *outbound*: involves proactive **marketing** in which prospective and pre-existing customers are contacted directly;
- *inbound*: involves the reception of incoming orders and requests for information which have been generated by **advertising, publicity** and **public relations**.

Teleological reasoning

The teleological approach to **ethics**, unlike **deontological reasoning**, emphasises outcomes. In other words, the ends justify the means. Restricted teleology calculates the consequences for a particular grouping (family or organisation). Universal teleology or **utilitarianism** stresses the consequences of any actions for society as a whole, (the greatest good for the greatest number). There are obvious ethical considerations with regard to any **public relations programme/plan**, especially those concerning **corporate social responsibility**.

Kohlberg (1984) suggested six stages of moral reasoning for **public relations** practitioners:

1. Individuals act out of fear of reprisal, obey the rules and comply with management orders.

2 Individuals exploit situations for personal gain and reward. They use manipulation and deception to achieve their goals. Short-term rewards are emphasised over the long- term consequences. This stage of moral reasoning falls within Grunig's model of **press agentry**.

3 Individuals practising this stage of reasoning conform to expected standards and actively promote the interests of their culture and organisation.

4 Individuals practising this stage obey the letter of the law. Correct action allows the group to function. Practitioners employing this reasoning would rely on written codes such as the **Code of Professional Conduct** of the **Chartered Institute of Public Relations (CIPR)** because they represent legitimate authority within the profession. This stage of moral reasoning falls within Grunig's model of **two-way symmetrical public relations**.

5 This stage is universal teleology or **utilitarianism**, where the consequences of any actions for society as a whole are paramount in any ethical decision.

6 This stage is principled reasoning, where any decisions are made on universal principles such as fairness, equity and justice and where people are seen as an end in themselves and not as a means to an end.

Kohlberg, L. (1984) *Essays on Moral Development,* Vol. 2, The Psychology of Moral Development: Moral Stages, their Nature and Validity. San Francisco: Harper and Row.

Parsons, P. (2004) *Ethics in Public Relations: A Guide to Best Practice.* London: Kogan Page.

Telephone interviews

Telephone interviews are a method of collating information cheaply and efficiently for **research** purposes.

Teletext and Ceefax

Teletext and Ceefax were developed in the UK in the early 1970s. They are television information-retrieval services, offering a wide range of text-based information, including national, international and sporting news, the weather, TV schedules, stock exchange prices, traffic conditions and opportunities for booking travel. Both of these services will be phased out after the full switchover to digital television in 2012.

www.teletext.co.uk
www.ceefax.tv

T

Tendering

Tendering means having to shop around for the best possible price for the best services or goods. Simple tenders may only involve repeat buying; more complex tendering might involve long-term arrangements. Tendering is also known as '**pitch**ing'. In **public relations**, practitioners **pitch** their ideas and concepts for a **public relations programme/plan** to a prospective client. Being awarded a contract or winning a **pitch** means that the **public relations** team or individual practitioner has been selected from tenders. They will then be given a contract detailing all the requirements, both legal and creative, of the project.

Testimonial

A testimonial is an **endorsement** by a third party of a product or service and is used as a **promotion**al device. Testimonials given by celebrities or other leading figures are often used as a **public relations tactic**.

Think tanks

Think tanks are part and parcel of **political communication**. They are made up of individuals who are politically motivated and theoretically driven, who develop options and challenging ideas for debate. They are unaccountable and discreet and their prime reason for being is to influence informal or social environments in which lobbyists engage with political elites. Some current examples of think tanks include:

- Adam Smith Institute
- Aims of Industry
- Bow Group
- Centre for Policy Studies
- Chatham House
- Commonwealth Policy Studies Institute
- Civitas
- Demos
- Fabian Society
- Foreign Policy Centre
- Globalisation Institute
- Institute for Public Policy Research
- Localis
- New Economics Foundation

T

- New Policy Institute
- New Politics Network
- Open Europe
- Reform
- Royal United Services for Defence Studies

The role of think-tank organisations is akin to that of management consultants and although there are many different types serving diverse niches, their impact on policy decisions is debatable.

Timescales

See **critical path analysis, Gantt chart.**

Tools

See **techniques, task-oriented structure.**

Trade Descriptions Act 1968

The Trade Descriptions Act 1968 is a UK Act of Parliament which prevents manufacturers, retailers or service industry providers from misleading consumers as to what they are buying. This law empowers the judiciary to punish companies or individuals who make false claims about a product or service.

See **crisis by criticism.**

www. tradingstandards.gov.uk

Trade fairs

Trade fairs are similar to **exhibitions** but are normally restricted to trade. Trade fairs are a vital forum for **business-to-business (B2B) public relations**.

See **exhibitions.**

Trade journal

A trade journal is a magazine or periodical intended to communicate with the target market of a specific trade or industry. They have a specific topical focus, with news and views on the industry in question and usually a selection of job vacancy notices. The trade journal for the **public relations** industry is called *PR Week* and is published by Haymarket. Contents usually concern the public and voluntary sector, **public affairs**, healthcare, city and corporate **public relations**, **media relations**, news **analysis**, profiles, opinions, campaigns and jobs.

PR Week, Haymarket Publishing.

Transparency

Transparency in **public relations** is a vital method of preventing conflicts of interest and the accusation of concealing information. The **Code of Professional Conduct** of the **Chartered Institute of Public Relations (CIPR)** states that integrity, competence, transparency and **confidentiality** are fundamental to good **public relations**. **Public relations** practitioners should:

- disclose to employers, clients or potential clients any financial interest in a supplier being recommended or engaged;
- declare conflicts of interests (or circumstances which may give rise to them) in writing to clients, potential clients and employers as soon as they arise;
- ensure that services provided are costed and accounted for in a manner which conforms to accepted business practice and **ethics**.

Trend analysis

Trend analysis is used to predict future events and refers to the concept of collecting information, facts and statistics to enable the analysts to spot trends or patterns. In **public relations**, trend analysis can be used to predict future communication behaviours or purchasing decisions. **Public relations** practitioners are then able to take account of these trends in their forward planning.

T

Two-way symmetrical communication

See **symmetrical communication**.

Unique selling proposition (USP)

The unique selling proposition (or unique selling point) is the main benefit of a product or service. It is the thing which gives the product or service added value, the thing which no other product has, the thing which makes one product more special or desirable than another. In other words, this single feature becomes the focus of the selling **message**.

Forte, A. (2002) *Dare to be Different: How to Create Business Advantage through Innovation and Unique Selling Proposition*. Weston-super-Mare: Forte Financial Group.

Uses and gratifications

The basic tenet of the uses and gratifications theory is that people use media texts for certain gratifications. The principle is that people are not passive consumers of media texts and information, but that they use the media to fulfil their particular needs. Jay Blumler and Elihu Katz devised their uses and gratifications model in 1974 to emphasise four areas of gratification in media texts for **audience**s. These include:

- *Escapism*: a media text can provide escapism by temporarily subsuming a reader's senses, e.g. when playing a video game.
- *Personal identity*: people can arrange their own identities through those who influence them from media texts, e.g. when readers are influenced by other people's ideas of **values**, norms, **ideologies**, fashions, thoughts and feelings.
- *Personal relationships*: readers of media texts can create personal relationships with the characters portrayed, both real and imagined. This impedes their ability to make objective judgments and they may be in danger of taking everything said by a person in a media text at face value.
- *Surveillance*: the **audience** gains an awareness and understanding of the world around it by consuming what is chosen

to be portrayed in media texts. However, it is important to remember that all writers, **journalist**s and authors structure their own reality. What appears to be 'real' and of value to one may not be so for another. Put simply, the media may be a source of entertainment, a place to find items of personal interest, a diversion from everyday life, a substitute for social relationships or a support for personal **value**s. The **public relations** practitioner is therefore likely to be concerned about the likely effectiveness of their output and to consider this in their **media planning**. More important than *where* to place **messages** is their effect and *how* these **messages** will be used.

Gillespie, M. and Toynbee, J. (eds) (2006) *Analysing Media Texts*. Maidenhead: Oxford University Press.

Utilitarianism

Utilitarianism can be contrasted with **deontological ethics**, which tends to focus on actions themselves rather than the consequences. Utilitarianism is often described by the phrase 'the greatest good for the greatest number', suggesting that the moral worth of an action is determined by its action. In other words, the ends justify the means. In **public relations**, utilitarian **ethics** have their place when considering the rationale for a **corporate social responsibility** programme.

Act utilitarianism states that if a person or group of people have a choice, they must consider the likely consequences of any potential actions and then choose the action they believe will generate the most happiness. *Rule utilitarianism* begins by examining potential rules of action and exploring what the outcome would be if these rules were always followed. If adhering to the rule produces more happiness than not, then this rule should be followed at all times. Ultimately, the distinction between act utilitarianism and rule utilitarianism is whether the most happiness is produced when attached specifically to a case or to a general rule.

The main criticism of utilitarianism is that a comparison of happiness among different types of people is almost impossible to measure, and the consequences of utilitarianism can be difficult for **public relations** practitioners to predict, which leads to speculation. Although utilitarianism advocates respect for individual preferences, the final decision has to be in the interests of the majority.

Unfortunately, utilitarianism does not allow for motive – which is important when thinking about morality – nor does it explain why some moral rules should not be broken, despite the consequences.

See **deontological reasoning, ethics, teleological reasoning.**

www.utilitarian.net
www.utilitarianism.com

U

Values

Values are subjective judgments of worth. There are neither right nor wrong, neither true nor false.

See **attitudes, beliefs.**

Value-adding

Contemporary **public relations** should move beyond thinking about its role of relationship-building and move towards its new role of adding value. The new business model of **public relations** demands that it be accountable and that it contribute to the net worth of an organisation. An efficient way of enabling added value is to emphasise less command and control within an organisation and more shared responsibility and individual accountability, including joint ventures and partnerships with other organisations or the **not-for-profit** sector. Running **public relations** departments as a proactive business means establishing value propositions and setting financial goals, such as revenue and profitability targets. In reality, this means letting go of such measuring yardsticks as column inches acquired by the organisation's latest accomplishments and relying more on helping the organisation to meet its business **objectives** by providing innovative, cost-effective communication **resources**.

Video blog (vlog)

A vlog is a **blog** consisting of video. Regular entries are presented in reverse chronological order and combine embedded video clips or a video link with supporting text- and image- based material.

Bryant, S. C. (2006) *Videoblogging for Dummies*. Hoboken, NJ: Wiley.

Video news release (VNR)

A VNR is a video version of a paper **press release** or **news release**. It is a segment of news which is filmed and then sent to a television news station for **public relations** purposes. One of the criticisms of VNRs is that the producers can construct their own reality by creating fake news which appears real, for example when an actor is used to appear as an average 'man in the street' but delivers perfectly scripted comments. This can present ethical problems.

Virtual community

A virtual community is also known as an e-community or an on-line community. It consists of a group of people who, for social, educational or professional purposes, interact and communicate electronically rather than face to face. The infiltration of virtual communities and the seeding of information can be used for **marketing** and **public relations** purposes. Some **public relations** practitioners set up their own virtual communities in order to engender debate about a specific **issue**, product or service, etc.

Hagel, J. and Armstrong, A. (1997) *Net Gain: Expanding Markets through Virtual Communities*. Boston: Harvard Business School Press.

Virtual press office

Many **journalist**s rely on the internet to source information and it is the responsibility of the **public relations** practitioner to supply that information through a virtual press office. Typical content of a virtual press office would include company information such as **backgrounders** and biographies, product information, **news release**s, **images** and contact details. **Press release**s should be searchable by client/product or key words and should be indexed in date order. The virtual press office should be accessible and regularly updated.

Visual identity

The visual identity of an organisation is the sum of the visual cues which enable the public to recognise the company and differentiate it from other companies. It is the visible element of the corporate **strategy** and incorporates such things as the **logo** and other physical presentations, such as the organisation's standard layouts, typography, colour schemes and interior design. Visual identity is also known as **organisational symbolism**.

Baldwin, J. and Roberts, L. (2006) *Visual Communication from Theory to Practice*, Lausanne: AVA.

V

Ww

Web surveys

Web surveys are used as a **research** tool in **public relations**. They can be designed to be part of a larger **website** or to stand alone. Web surveys are considered to have several advantages in that they are fast, effective and cost-efficient. They also allow for the inclusion of **graphics**, colour and creative formatting, which can increase the web survey's appeal.

Website

The first on-line website appeared in 1991. On 30 April 1993 the World Wide Web became free for everyone. Since that date there has been a massive explosion of internet travel and the proliferation of websites as **public relations tools** has increased beyond all expectations. Websites are important because they represent an organisation's **image** and **brand values** online and can be used to communicate cost-effectively with many types of **audience**. **Public relations** practitioners are often asked to help their clients set up their own websites and should at least be aware of how to edit material on the web.

Websites may be used as:

- *business-to-business (B2B) tools*: communicating with third parties, shareholders, potential investors, industry bodies, analysts, trade media, etc;
- *business-to-consumer (B2C) tools*: communicating with customers, both existing and potential, through information **resources**, e-commerce, entertainment, portals, etc;
- *internal communication **tools***: providing specific information to staff, clients and affiliates using **intranet**s, extranets and password-protected areas on corporate sites.

According to Kirsner (1998), a successful website should have the following features:

- a 'What's new' section so that users can identify the latest content and go directly to it;

- a search engine or site map to ensure that all content is easy to find;
- a **feedback** mechanism, either an on-line form or an e-mail address, so that users can comment on the site and content and suggest areas for improvement;
- consistent navigation;
- security information;
- linking instructions in order to encourage reciprocal links with other relevant organisations;
- a privacy policy;
- location and contact details.

Kirsner, S. (1998) 'Must haves' on CIO Web Business Magazine, (www.cio. com), Aug.

White paper

A white paper is a **promotion**al piece in the guise of an informational **article** or report. A white paper tries to convince readers that they are being educated about the **issue** or problem that the product addresses. The white paper serves the same sales purpose as a **brochure** but it reads or looks like an authoritative **article** and takes a more 'soft-sell' approach.

See **on-line copywriting assignments.**

Willings Press Guide

Willings Press Guide is a directory in several volumes of press contacts, target **audience** information, **advertising** rates and **e-zine**s and contact information in Europe, Eastern Europe, China, the USA and South American countries. The three volumes – UK, Western Europe and World – have clear and easy-to-use referencing, **website** and **broadcast media** information.

www.willingspress.com

W

Win–win

A win–win situation is a process of **negotiation** whereby the interacting parties find a solution which **benefits** them both. A win–win–no-deal situation is where the parties cannot find a solution which **benefits** them both and so they agree to disagree – no deal.

See **game theory, negotiation.**

Xx

XPRL (extensible public relations language)

XPRL is an open specification for an extensible mark-up language (XML) being developed for the **public relations** industry. The aim of the UK-based XPRL initiative group is to standardise the way in which industry-specific computer data is stored and shared over the internet. According to the XPRL steering group, the new schema-based mark-up language will benefit not only **public relations** professionals but also anyone dealing with that business sector, including **journalist**s, content aggregators and **public relations** management. Developers can use XPRL to write automated **public relations** tasks. For example when an on-line version of a **press release** is written, tags will be generated which identify document components, such as images, **headlines**, dates, etc. Each version of the document can be identified and changes can be automatically tracked and managed. Consequently, any cutting agency will be able automatically to capture copy for delivery to clients.

Yardstick model

Lindenmann's **public relations** yardstick model (1993) aimed to make **evaluation** more accessible. He claimed that **public relations evaluation** need be neither expensive nor laboriously time-consuming. The yardstick model consists of a two-step process:

1 setting **public relations objectives**;
2 determining at what level **public relations** effectiveness is to be measured.

Three levels gauge the extent of measurement;

1 This is the basic level which measures **public relations** outputs such as **media relations**. Here the measurement is in terms of media placements and the likelihood of reaching the target **audience**.
2 This is the intermediate level which uses 'outgrowth' measures to show whether **audiences** actually receive the **messages** and evaluates retention, understanding and awareness. **Public relations** practitioners will use differing **quantitative** and **qualitative** data-collection **techniques**, such as **focus groups** and **interviews**.
3 This level measures 'outcomes', which can include opinions, **attitudes** and changes in behaviour.

Lindenmann, W. K. (1993) 'An "effectiveness yardstick" to measure public relations success', *Public Relations Quarterly*, 38, 1, 7–9.

Zero-time communication environment

Public relations operates in a zero-time communication environment in that the rapid and readily changing advances in technology are resulting in instant global communications. Not only is this communication space instantaneous, it also allows for direct and rapid competition with other significant role-players in the local and global economies.

See **globalisation.**

Zones of influence

Stone (1995) quotes **research** from the 1970s which identifies six main zones of influence within families when making buying decisions. These are:

- man
- woman
- children
- man and woman
- man and children
- woman and children.

This was followed by later **research** in 1991 which suggested that women were dominant in the purchase of household goods. Information on buying decisions can inform the **public relations** practitioner when planning campaigns and selecting the appropriate **tactics** to carry **messages** about particular products to specific **audience**s.

Stone, N. (1995) *The Management and Practice of Public Relations*. London: Macmillan Business.

Index